CULTURES OF THE WORLD

BURMA

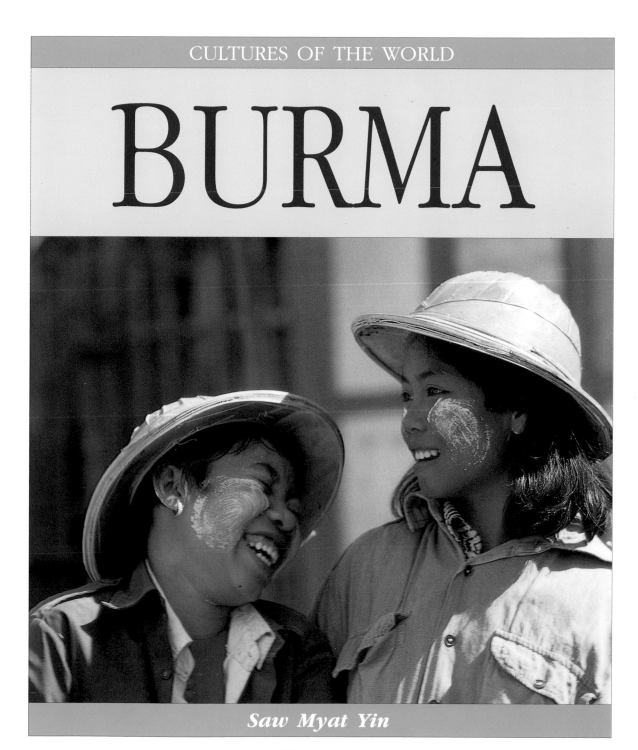

Saw Myat Yin

MARSHALL CAVENDISH
New York • London • Sydney

Editorial Director	Shirley Hew
Managing Editors	Mark Dartford
	Shova Loh
Editors	Goh Sui Noi
	Meena Mylvaganam
	Cheryl M. English
Picture Editor	Jane Duff
Production	Jeremy Chan
	Robert Paulley
	Julie Cairns
Design	Tuck Loong
	Doris Nga
	Stella Liu
	Lee Woon Hong
Illustrators	Francis Oak
	Thomas Koh
	Vincent Chew

Reference edition published 1990 by
Marshall Cavendish Corporation
147 West Merrick Road
Freeport, Long Island
N.Y. 11520

Printed in Singapore by
Kim Hup Lee Printing Co. Pte Ltd

Originated and designed by
Times Books International
an imprint of Times Editions Pte Ltd
Times Center, 1 New Industrial Road
Singapore 1953
Telex: 37908 EDTIME Fax: 2854871

Library of Congress Cataloging-in-Publication Data:
Yin, Saw Myat, 1946–
      Burma / by Saw Myat Yin.
        p. cm.—(Cultures of the world)
      Includes bibliographical references.
      Summary: Introduces the geography,
      history, religious beliefs, government, and
      people of Burma.
      ISBN 1-85435-299-1: $19.95
      1. Burma—Juvenile literature. [1. Burma.]
I. Title. II. Series.
DS527.4.Y56 1990
959.1—dc20   89-25463
                       CIP
                       AC

INTRODUCTION

BURMA, or Union of Myanmar as it is now officially named, is a country little known to the rest of the world, even to its Asian neighbors. For more than a quarter century it has been so isolated as to have almost disappeared from the map   of the world.

People who have heard of Burma know it as "the land of pagodas" or as "the land where time has stopped," somewhere around 1940. Yet there is more to Burma than pagodas, and life is rich in this place where "time has stopped." Outside the pagodas are colorful bazaars where people throng to buy or just to look at the wares, many handcrafted. Whether country folk or urbanites, Burmese have time to sit around a pot of tea and exchange tall tales or the latest jokes. Or find an occasion to make a feast so that friends and relatives can gather.

This book, part of the series Cultures of the World, explores this little known country whose history dates back more than nine hundred years, where the lifestyle and customs of the people have remained relatively unchanged over many centuries.

Myitkyina

Maymyo

Mandalay

Pagan

Taunggyi

Toungoo

Prome

Pegu

Rangoon

Moulmein

Tavoy

Mergui

CONTENTS

An old Karen couple enjoying a smoke.

CONTENTS

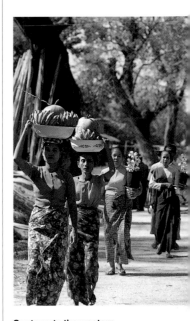

Contrary to the western image of Asian women as retiring, Burmese women are independent and active outside the home. Bazaars are almost entirely run by women who seem to have a flair for business.

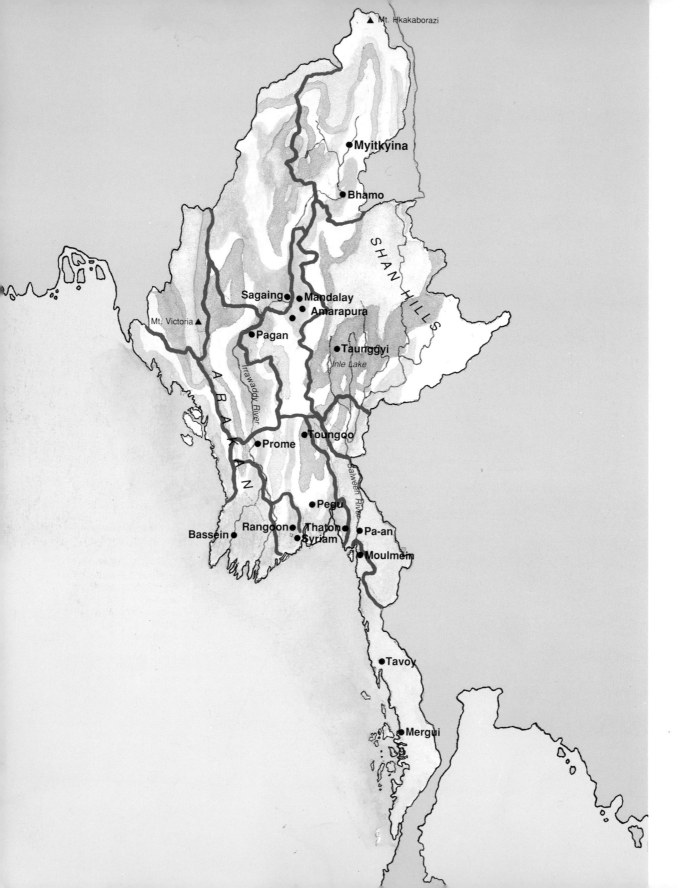

GEOGRAPHY

GEOGRAPHICAL LOCATION

BURMA lies in mainland Southeast Asia, bordered by India in the northwest, Bangladesh and the Bay of Bengal in the west, the Andaman Sea in the southwest, China in the north, and Laos and Thailand in the east.

Apart from a 1,400-mile-long coastline, Burma is surrounded by a horseshoe-shaped ring of mountains which forms a natural border of almost 4,000 miles with her neighbors. The main rivers are the Irrawaddy, Chindwin, Salween and Sittang. The country, about the size of the state of Texas, covers 262,000 square miles and consists of the seven states of Arakan (or Rakhine), Chin, Kachin, Karen, Kayah, Shan, Mon, and seven divisions of Rangoon, Mandalay, Magwe, Sagaing, Pegu, Irrawaddy and Tenasserim.

Burma is a rural country where cities with a population of over 100,000 number only eight. There were about 65,000 villages in the 1980s.

Burma is still largely rural, with many Burmese living in villages surrounded by rolling green hills and paddy fields.

SEASONS

Burma has three seasons, the rainy season, or monsoon, from July to October, a cool season from November to February, and a hot season from March to June. Rainfall is up to 200 inches in the coastal regions, 100 inches in the plains and an average of 29 inches in the central part. The highest temperature is 113°F in central Burma, and the lowest, 32°F, in the north. The average annual temperature vary from 71°F in the highlands of the Shan plateau to 81°F in the southern lowlands.

The Arakan Yoma, or "Arakan main bone," in the distance, is part of the western ranges and separates the Arakan coastal strip from the central plain.

NORTHERN AND WESTERN REGION

Burma can roughly be divided into four regions: northern and western mountainous region, the central belt, the eastern Shan plateau and the long southern "tail."

The northern and western mountains extend from the extreme north down to the western side of Burma. Kachin, Chin and Arakan States are located in this region. Some of Burma's highest peaks are here: Mt. Hkakaborazi (19,296 ft), the highest in Southeast Asia, and Mt. Gamlanrazi, both in the extreme north and part of the Kachin range; and Mt. Sarameti and Mt. Victoria in the Chin range.

Arakan State in the west has a coastal strip which is wide in the north and narrows toward the south. The resort beaches are located here. Offshore, numerous islands dot the Bay of Bengal.

The vegetation in this region varies from tropical and subtropical to temperate and alpine, with an abundance of rhododendron, magnolia, juniper, pine, birch and cherry. Bamboo forests cover a large area of the Arakan range; wild animals still survive here in the mountains—bears, civet cats, elephants, leopards and tigers. The rare takin, red panda, tapir, snow leopard and musk deer are found in the northern temperate region.

The capitals of Kachin, Chin and Arakan States are Myitkyina, Falam and Akyab respectively.

Coconut palms favor the sandy soil of the Arakan coast.

The rich plains of the central region are the rice bowl of Burma, with acres and acres of land devoted to rice-planting.

CENTRAL REGION

The central region has a dry zone, but here are also the rich river valleys and plains of the mighty Irrawaddy, the Chindwin—a tributary of the Irrawaddy—and the Sittang. Low mountain ranges flank the river valleys.

In the dry zone the flora consists of thorny trees and shrubs and cacti. Snakes, especially poisonous vipers, abound here although snakes are found in the other regions. Petroleum and gas are produced here. Agricultural products such as beans, pulses,* cotton, onions, chilli, oilseeds and tobacco are also produced. Important cities in this area are Mandalay, Monywa, Magwe and Pakkoku.

Teak and other hardwoods cover the slopes of the mountain ranges, while in the river valleys and plains, the main crop is rice. Jute and sugar cane, important industrial raw materials, are also grown here. Fish and shrimp are bred in ponds and harvested from rivers and creeks.

The main cities in this area are: Rangoon, the capital; Bassein; Pegu, the ancient Mon capital, about 45 miles north of Rangoon; and Prome and Toungoo, also historical capitals.

* Pulses are edible seeds from leguminous plants such as peas and lentils.

10

BURMA'S LIFELINE

The Irrawaddy, Burma's lifeline, is 2,170 miles long. Its source is in the Himalayas and it flows down the middle of Burma to the Andaman Sea. It divides Burma into two; most of the towns are on the east bank. Burma's historical capitals are also on this side, capitals such as Mandalay, Ava, Amarapura, Prome and Pagan. Only one bridge, the Ava bridge near Mandalay, spans the Irrawaddy. All other crossings are made by ferries of all sizes and shapes, from large car ferries to narrow, long row boats.

The Irrawaddy is the backbone of the country's transport system. On this great river one can see steamers carrying passengers and cargo, barges on which families spend their entire lives, carrying products up and down the river, and great rafts of bamboo or teak floating down to Rangoon for export.

The delta in the south, where the river divides into eight main branches before flowing into the Andaman Sea, is Burma's "rice bowl." Here, the soil is fertile from annual flooding and alluvial deposits, and is suitable for rice cultivation. The delta covers 13,000 square miles and is a veritable network of streams and creeks. The delta area is famous for fish and shrimp and products derived from them.

Right: **The five-day bazaar is a market that moves from town to town around Taunggyi the capital of the Shan State, and the nearby towns of Heho, Kalaw, Shwenyaung and Yawnghwe. Vendors come from the villages around these towns and the bazaar is colorful and lively with Shan and other ethnic groups in their native dress.**

Below: **A delicate beauty, the blue vanda orchid is native to the Shan plateau.**

SHAN PLATEAU

The Shan plateau in eastern Burma is a tableland about 3,000 feet above sea level, and forms the border with China, Laos and Thailand. The Salween river, Burma's longest at 1,749 miles, rises in Tibet and flows down the plateau through narrow gorges. The Shan State is in the northern part of the plateau and Kayah State, in the southern part. The climate on the plateau is cool all the year round.

Pine and cherry trees grow wild here, so do many wild orchids, on trees and rocky clefts; the blue vanda orchid is a native of the Shan plateau. Mogok, in western Shan State, is famous for its rubies, sapphires and other gems. Lead, silver, tin, tungsten and marble are also obtained from this area.

Tea, fruit such as avocados, pears, oranges, tangerines and strawberries, and vegetables such as carrots, cabbages, kohlrabi, beans and peas, are cultivated here. Opium is grown in the part of the Shan State which is included in the Golden Triangle; here, the Shans fight a protracted war with the central government for autonomy.

TENASSERIM COASTAL STRIP

The Tenasserim coastal strip—comprising the states of Mon and Tenasserim—is the long "tail" of Burma which extends from the Shan plateau down to the Isthmus of Kra in the south. The mountain ranges to the left form a natural border with Thailand. Tin and tungsten are mined in this region, and forests are logged.

The only available agricultural land here is a narrow strip between the mountains and the sea. The land is well used with rice being the main crop. Numerous orchards grow fruit such as pineapple, durian, rambutan, mangosteen, cashew nut and coconut. Rubber is also grown here.

Offshore fishing and related industries such as canning and preserving are found in the towns of Tavoy and Mergui. The Tenasserim coast has a number of resort beaches but these are not accessible to foreigners.

The capitals of Mon State (Moulmein) and Tenasserim (Tavoy) are trading centers for goods which flow in from neighboring Thailand.

THE MERGUI ARCHIPELAGO The Mergui archipelago is a group of some 800 islands off the Tenasserim coast opposite the town of Mergui. The Salon people who live here are known as sea gypsies and are famous for deep-sea diving for pearls and abalone. They were once feared for piracy of vessels passing through their waters.

A "bus" in Moulmein, the capital of Mon State. Burmese ingenuity went to work to convert an old truck into a "bus," using the hardy teakwood which is plentiful in Burma.

In the villages bullock carts are still used as a means of transport, while in the cities, "pickup" trucks with a roof over the body, and benches installed, serve to supplement bus services run by the government. These vehicles are imported by Burmese who have gone abroad to study or work (see opposite page).

TRANSPORT

Burma's roads and railways follow the north-to-south physical arrangement of rivers and mountain ranges. East-to-west roads are few and cross mountain ranges through mountain passes. Rivers impede road travel and crossings are made by ferry. The roads and railways are a heritage from the British colonizers and further development has been slow due to economic stagnation and political isolation, which preclude international aid. Ethnic states remain as remote as before independence.

Rivers are important for trade and transportation, especially the Irrawaddy and Sittang rivers and their branches in the delta. River craft are mostly crowded, old private steamers. The northern portion of the Sittang and Salween rivers are not navigable but these rivers are useful as chutes for floating down teak, other hardwoods and bamboo after extraction from the forests.

Air transport has deteriorated because of lack of foreign exchange needed for new planes and spare parts.

CITIES

RANGOON Rangoon, recently renamed its Burmese name Yangon, is Burma's capital and main port. Founded in 1755 by King Alaungpaya, it grew into a trading port after the British annexed lower Burma in 1826, and became the capital after the whole of Burma fell under the British in 1890.

Rangoon, accessible to foreigners only by sea or air, is a quiet and green city with two large lakes. Highrise buildings are nonexistent; the tallest building is only six stories high. Being the capital, ministries, directorates and head offices of government organizations are located here, as are institutions of higher learning. The population, including that of the satellite towns of North and South Okkalapa and Thaketa, was over 4 million in 1987, with ethnic Burmese being the majority. The city population density was 1,013 persons per square mile.

On a Rangoon road, one finds old cars, tall, shady roadside trees, and no traffic jams.

THE SHWE DAGON

The Shwe Dagon, on Singuttara Hill in Rangoon, is Burma's most sacred pagoda. It enshrines Buddha's hair and other holy relics. Originally only 27 feet high, it is now 326 feet in height through successive renovations by kings and queens.

Gold and precious gems adorn the pagoda and are also buried in the main treasure chamber under the spire. Four staircases (each with about 130 steps) lead to the pagoda, which is surrounded by numerous smaller spires and monasteries. The main platform and surrounding terraces are always full of worshipers offering flowers, food, candles and water, meditating or telling beads.

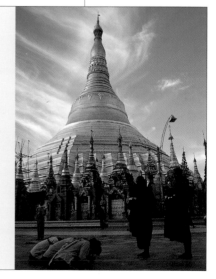

MANDALAY Mandalay is Burma's second largest city and the country's main cultural center. It lies on the east bank of the Irrawaddy, about 500 miles north of Rangoon. Established in 1857 by King Mindon, it was Burma's last capital before it came under British rule. The magnificent Mandalay palace was burned down during the Second World War and only a scale model remains in the palace grounds, which are surrounded by a moat. However, many ancient pagodas and monasteries still stand.

Mandalay is famous not only for being a center of Buddhist learning and fine arts, but also for its gold and silver crafts, carving and weaving. It has a population of 750,000 and is a trading center for agricultural and other products from all parts of upper Burma.

MOULMEIN Moulmein is the third largest city and is situated at the mouth of the Salween. It is an important port and trading center for products of the Tenasserim area and products that arrive overland from neighboring countries. Moulmein is famous for its fruits; the people are reputed to be gastronomes, and the women are said to possess great culinary skill.

BASSEIN Bassein, Burma's second largest port after Rangoon, is 28 miles from the sea on the Bassein River. It has a population of 150,000, and is famous for rice, fish and shrimp, their derived products, and colorful handpainted parasols.

Mandalay is also described as the religious heart of Burma, and here, many craftsmen ply trades which are related to religion. Workshops turn out all kinds of religious objects and pagoda ornaments including umbrellas which are offered to Buddha images or venerated monks as a special honor.

PAGAN

Pagan is situated on the east bank of the Irrawaddy, about 120 miles south of Mandalay. Its 16 square miles are covered by countless pagodas and temples from the 11th century onward, some in ruins and some in gilded splendor.

Pagan was first established as a walled city in A.D. 849. Beginning from Anawrahta's reign in 1044, Pagan became a powerful kingdom stretching to Bhamo in the north, Salween in the east, Assam, Arakan and the Chin hills in the west, and the Mon kingdom in the south. Anawrahta conquered the Mon people and brought to Pagan the king and royal family, artisans, craftsmen —and Theravada Buddhism, which flourished under successive kings who built many pagodas in religious fervor. The architecture, frescoes, murals, plaster carvings and bas-reliefs of these pagodas have been described as marvelous relics of Pagan's glory. Pagan fell to the Mongols in 1287 and most of the temples are said to have been pulled down by the Burmese in an attempt to fortify themselves.

Many pagodas were destroyed by an earthquake in 1975 but international agencies have helped in restoration work. Pagan's dry climate, probably resulting from excessive felling of trees for firewood to feed brick kilns where pagoda bricks were made, has helped to preserve these precious monuments.

HISTORY

HISTORICAL CHRONOLOGY

849	Founding of Pagan
1057	King Anawrahta (1044–1077) defeats the Mons and unifies the country under the First Burmese Empire.
1084	King Kyanzittha (1084–1112), Anawratha's son, is elected to the throne. The golden age of pagoda-building at Pagan begins.
1287	The Mongols, under Kublai Khan, conquer Pagan and the Burmese empire falls.
1541	King Tabinshwehti of Toungoo (1531–1551) conquers the Mon capital of Pegu and much of central Burma.
1558	King Bayinnaung, Tabinshwehti's successor, founds the Second Burmese Empire and extends control over Chiang Mai and, later, the whole Chao Phraya valley. After his death, the kingdom gradually falls apart.
1755	King Alaungpaya (1752–1760) founds the Third Burmese Empire at Shwebo, north of present-day Mandalay.
1767	King Hsinbyushin (1763–1776) destroys the Siamese capital of Ayuthia, taking many captives who strongly influence Burmese arts.
1783	King Bodawpaya annexes Arakan and brings the Burmese border up against British India.
1824	The first Anglo-Burmese war breaks out. Burma is defeated and cedes Arakan and Tenasserim to the British.
1852	The second Anglo-Burmese war breaks out. Burma is defeated and the British take control of lower Burma.
1885	Led by King Thibaw, Burma goes to war with the British for a third and last time. King Thibaw is exiled to India and Burma is ruled as part of British India.
1906	The first significant nationalist organization of the 20th century, the Young Men's Buddhist Association, is formed.
1930	The All Burma Student Movement, opposed to British rule, is founded.
1937	Burma is separated from India and now has a new constitution and its own legislative council.
1943	Burma is declared independent under Japanese military occupation.
1945	The Japanese surrender in August.
1948	British grants independence to Burma. The Union of Burma becomes a nation under Prime Minister U Nu.
1962	General Ne Win comes into power following a military coup and Burma closes its door to the world.
1974	The Socialist Republic of the Union of Burma is created after Ne Win disbands the revolutionary council and introduces a new constitution.
1988	Student-led demonstrations lead to a military coup; the military government declares that Burma is no longer on a socialist path.
1989	Burma is renamed Union of Myanmar.

It was only after the establishment of the First Burmese Empire in 1057 that Burma became a distinct political entity.

Opposite: **An 11th century terracotta plaque, inscribed in Mon language, tells a *Jataka* tale, or a story about the Buddha before his enlightenment.**

PREHISTORY

The Irrawaddy valley was inhabited some five thousand years ago by the Anyathians, hunters and gatherers who used stone and wood tools. Further north in the eastern part of the Shan State, cave paintings and stone tools show that there were also early settlers here. However, the Anyathians and the Shan cave people stayed far from the sea. The earliest settlers on the coast were the Negritos who had come from Indonesia.

A burial urn from the prehistoric period, found in Sri Kshetra, Upper Burma.

ARRIVAL OF THE FIRST BURMANS

A few centuries before Christ, the Mons entered Burma from the region of what are now Thailand and Cambodia, and settled around the mouths of the Salween and Sittang rivers. They cultivated and exported rice, as well as teak, minerals and ivory, to India, Arabia, China and Indochina.

At about the same time, some Tibeto-Burmese tribes, including the Pyus and their allied tribes, left their homeland on the southeastern slopes of the Tibetan plateau and migrated south, entering the Upper Irrawaddy valley. The Pyus, a loosely knit group of tribes who disappeared in the 8th century, were the first migrants to found a great kingdom, at Prome. Devout Theravada Buddhists, the Pyus were a graceful people. Some centuries later, the Pyus were pushed back by the Mons. In the process, the Burmans, a people hitherto subject to the Pyus, rose to prominence.

In the 12th century A.D., the Shans, also known as Tais, arrived from Yunnan, northeast of Burma. The Burmans of today are descendants of these races, the Mons, the Burmans, the Pyus, and the Shans.

FIRST BURMESE EMPIRE (1044-1257)

After the Pyus were pushed north by the Mons, the Burmans had established a small settlement of their own and founded the city of Pagan in A.D. 849. After many dynastic struggles during the first two centuries of Pagan's existence, Anawrahta, a Burman military leader, became king of Pagan in A.D. 1044. During his thirty-three years as ruler, he conquered the Mons, brought Buddhism to Pagan, and united all of modern Burma except for the Shan plateau and parts of Arakan and Tenasserim. His reign was known as the First Burmese Empire and marked the beginning of Burma as a distinct political entity. The kingdom survived until 1287, when it fell before the armies of Kublai Khan; for the next three centuries disunity characterized Burma which had disintegrated into small states.

Taking advantage of the ensuing turmoil after the fall of the First Burmese Empire, the Mons moved south and founded a new kingdom in Pegu in lower Burma. The Shans also broke away and extended their territory westward, establishing a capital in Ava on the banks of the Irrawaddy. The remaining Burmans withdrew to Toungoo on the river of Sittang to await an opportunity to initiate the reunification of Burma.

The First Burmese Empire was established by King Anawrahta after many wars, marking the beginning of Burma as a distinct political entity.

SECOND BURMESE EMPIRE (1551–1752)

The Burmans under King Tabinshwehti (1531–1551) in 1541 took advantage of the frequent wars between the Shans and Mons and captured Ava and Pegu. After his death, however, the kingdom again fell apart.

His brother-in-law and successor, King Bayinnaung (1551–1581), later not only reconquered all the lost territory but also won Chiang Mai and Ayuthia from the Siamese and took back Tenasserim, thus founding the Second Burmese Empire. Other states on the Burmese-Chinese border, and Manipur, now part of India, paid tribute to Burma.

During this period, trade with neighboring countries developed; Pegu became an important port for traders traveling to China via the Irrawaddy and northern Burma. It was also a convenient stop for traders going to other parts of Southeast Asia by way of Syriam, Martaban and Bassein, which were important ports in lower Burma.

Foreigners, especially Arabs and Portuguese, were very active in east-west trade. The British, French and Dutch trading companies were established in Burma in the 17th century when the capital was moved from Pegu to Ava. During the 18th century, Ava's rule became weaker, and the Mons, with help from the French, captured it in 1752.

THIRD BURMESE EMPIRE (1752–1885)

After conquering Ava, the Mons tried to control all Burma until the Burman headman of a tiny Shwebo village tract, Alaungpaya, defeated them. After eight years of wars, King Alaungpaya was able to unite the country again and founded the Konbaung Dynasty, the third and last Burmese empire. He also moved the capital back to Ava.

Hsinbyushin, Alaungpaya's son and successor, invaded Siam and destroyed Ayuthia in 1767. As a result, Tenasserim was again under Burmese control. This victory brought to Burma Siamese dancers, musicians and artisans who influenced Burmese art and literature. Another development during this period was the conquest of Arakan by Hsinbyushin's brother, Bodawpaya. During his reign, Bodawpaya improved the tax collection, communications, legal and educational systems.

During this dynasty, with few exceptions, the death of a king was followed by assassinations and rebellions. The lack of a system for appointing a successor to the throne was one of the reasons for the disunity among the Burmese which resulted in the eventual fall of the dynasty.

The Mandalay court of the last Burmese king, Thibaw. Founded by King Mindon, Mandalay was formally inaugurated as the capital in 1859.

King Thibaw fought the third and last war with the British, and lost. He was exiled to India and his dominions claimed by the victors.

BRITISH RULE (1886–1942)

In 1886, after three wars with the British, Burma became a British colony. The three Anglo-Burmese wars in 1824, 1852 and 1886 had their origin in British economic and political interests in Burma.

After the first war Burma lost Arakan and Tenasserim. In 1852 the British annexed lower Burma in order to close the gap between Calcutta and Singapore, and made it a province of British India. In 1885, Burma tried to make contact with the outside world, especially France, during the reign of the last king, Thibaw. The British, fearing French interference and wanting a monopoly in teak, used a dispute between Burma and a British timber firm, accused of illegal logging, as an excuse to march to Mandalay, the capital. In 1886 all of Burma became a province of British India, and the royal family was exiled to India.

The British introduced the classic divide-and-rule principle, giving the minority states permission to be ruled by their own leaders. They did not recruit Burmese for their army. All important posts in the civil service were filled by Indians or other foreigners. Burma's natural resources were exploited by foreigners and profits channeled out of the country. The British allowed Indians to migrate to Burma to alleviate labor shortage in the rice fields. All these factors inspired the Burmese nationalists to rebel against the British.

In the early 20th century, the nationalist movement, under the leadership of the Young Men's Buddhist Association (YMBA) and Rangoon University student leaders, grew from strength to strength. During the Second World War, Aung San, the national hero, led the struggle against the British, and the Japanese who occupied the country during the war. After the war the British finally gave Burma its independence.

This 19th century print shows British soldiers in the Shwe Dagon—complete with army boots. A strict rule of the Burmese is that footwear must be removed before entering temple grounds.

GENERAL AUNG SAN

General Aung San is Burma's national hero and the father of Burma's independence. He started his political career as a young student leader at Rangoon University, initiating the Thakin movement together with other students. The members of this movement, dissatisfied with having to address the British as Thakin—meaning "master"—feeling that this demeaned the Burmese, termed themselves Thakin and wore traditional Burmese clothes.

When the Second World War came, Aung San formed the Thirty Comrades, a group of thirty young men who swore a blood oath. They secretly went to Japan to ask for help and training to remove the British from Burma. The Japanese, however, proved to be ruthless when they came. Towards the end of the Second World War , Aung San and his Burma Independence Army sought the help of the British to drive out the Japanese.

After the war, Aung San continued to negotiate for independence, which was won on January 4, 1948. However, he did not live to see the day: aged only thirty-two, he was assassinated, together with six cabinet ministers, on July 19, 1947.

AFTER INDEPENDENCE

After independence the country remained unsettled with insurrections from the minorities who wanted their own autonomous states and from the communists who had chosen to go underground. Indeed these insurrections continue to this day, more than forty years after independence.

Elections which should have been held soon after independence were held only in 1951 after the army had managed to contain the insurgency problem and regained control of the country. In this election the Anti-Fascist People's Freedom League (AFPFL) won. This political party was an offshoot of the Anti-Fascist Organization, a secret party formed during the Japanese occupation.

The insurgency problem continued to plague the new government. Economic development plans were implemented but without much success. Export earnings fell due to the decline of rice export earnings and domestic revenue collection was hampered by the insurrections.

In the late 1950s, with the economy floundering, the AFPFL split into two groups, the "Clean" and the "Stable." As a result of armed clashes in the villages, a caretaker government was asked to take over in 1958. The caretaker government consisted of members of the armed forces. During the two years of the caretaker government the economy improved, the capital of Rangoon became cleaner, and the government departments more efficient.

Elections were held in 1960 to return the country to civil rule. The "Clean" AFPFL, now known as the Pyidaungsu Party, won. However, the insurrection problem became more severe as the Shans wanted secession.

On March 2, 1962, the army once more stepped in and took over the government in a *coup d'état*. The military government, known as the Revolutionary Government, had as its highest body the Revolutionary Council, composed of 17 high-ranking members of the Armed Forces. The government declared its socialist aims, abolishing democracy. The country embarked on a policy of withdrawal and isolation, a self-sufficient economy and strict neutrality in world politics.

Soon after it came to power widespread nationalization of trading organizations, banks, industries, schools and hospitals took place. Many foreigners were obliged to leave.

In 1974 a new constitution was adopted after a national referendum. The country became known as the Socialist Republic of the Union of Burma and the Burma Socialist Programme Party was the only political party allowed.

In 1988, student-led demonstrations led to a military coup. The new government, formed by the State Law and Order Council, changed the official title of the country to the Union of Myanmar in 1989 and declared that the country was no longer on the socialist path.

Luyechun are welcomed by the local working people. In 1964, the Ministry of Education began the *luyechun* scheme in which promising young people, selected among students in schools, colleges and universities, were nurtured for future leadership.

GOVERNMENT

MILITARY GOVERNMENT

BURMA is at present ruled by a military government which came to power after a *coup d'état* on September 18, 1988.

Prior to this, the government had been a socialist government with a one-party system of government. The Burma Socialist Programme Party, or BSPP, had based its policies on the Burmese Way to Socialism, a mixture of socialism and Buddhism, declared on April 30, 1962. In 1974, a new constitution was adopted and a new flag and state seal were introduced.

The government from this period up to the time of the coup consisted of the Pyithu Hluttaw, the parliament, with the Council of State and four subordinate organs of state power, the Council of Ministers, the Council of People's Justices, the Council of People's Attorneys and the Council of People's Inspectors. The Council of State was elected by the parliament; the Chairman of the Council of State was also the President of the Socialist Republic of the Union of Burma.

Left: **The Burmese state flag. The paddy and the cogwheel represent the peasants and workers who form the bulwark of the country while the 14 white stars denote unity and equal rights among the 14 states and divisions. White is for purity and cleanliness while the blue canton stands for peace and stability. Red signifies determination and courage.**

Opposite: **The Rangoon City Hall with the Independence Monument in the foreground.**

29

Students—some masked for protection, some bearing flags—take to the streets to demand for democracy.

POLITICAL UPHEAVAL

A series of political events throughout 1988 caused an upheaval in the country's government. The chief reason for political unrest was the impoverished state of the country caused by years of economic mismanagement, a prolonged insurgency problem and a heavy foreign debt. Beginning with student demonstrations in as early as 1987, the unrest spread to include the masses in Rangoon, Mandalay and other cities. The demonstrations became anarchic and violent throughout the months of July, August and September, 1988, and finally resulted in the *coup d'état* on September 18, 1988. Martial law was imposed immediately after the coup.

The country is at present governed by the State Law and Order Restoration Council (SLORC), with local governing bodies called State Law and Order Restoration Committees, at the state, division, township, township sector and ward levels.

UNION OF MYANMAR

Soon after the coup, the country was renamed Union of Burma, but has recently been given another name, the Union of Myanmar. Names of certain towns were also changed to their Burmese equivalents; Rangoon, the capital, was renamed Yangon.

The military government has promised that elections will be held in May 1990 and a large number of political parties (over 200) have registered with the General Elections Commission. The largest party, National League for Democracy is headed by Daw Aung San Suu Kyi, the daughter of General Aung San. However, as of December 1989, the capital, Rangoon (Yangon), was still under martial law with a nightly curfew, still in force after more than a year. Meetings and rallies have been banned so that the political parties do not yet have the chance to campaign in any way.

Daw Aung San Suu Kyi, daughter of national hero General Aung San, came home to Burma in April 1988 to care for her ailing mother, but soon became involved in a political upheaval.

In spite of the introduction of tractors (about 9,000) the great majority of farmers continue to use draft animals (6.8 million), mainly oxen and buffaloes, not only for plowing, but also to pull the bullock carts, and to thresh the grain or turn oil mills. Cow dung can be used for manure and, when dried, serves as a fuel source. Milk and beef are consumed by the population.

ECONOMY

MAIN OCCUPATIONS

BURMA is a largely rural country with more than 70% of the population living in rural areas and over two-thirds of the population dependent on agriculture for a living. Of the labor force of 16 million (1988/89), about 63% is estimated to be in agriculture. Nearly half of the gross domestic product (a measure of a country's produce) is from the primary sector, including agriculture, forestry, fishing and livestock-rearing. About 19.5 million acres are cultivated out of a total of 45.5 million acres of usable land; about 12 million acres are paddy fields.

FARMING

Unlike in the west, Burmese farmers do not live on individual farms but in villages surrounded by fields. There are over 14,000 village tracts in Burma. The farmers go out to the fields every day where they usually have small huts for resting and eating. Although technically all land is owned by the state, farmers own the land they work on to all intents and purposes.

The main areas for rice growing are the Irrawaddy Delta, the coastal regions of Arakan and Tenasserim, and the Sittang valley. Other areas also grow rice, but only for local consumption. Beans, pulses and oil seed are cultivated in the dry regions in central Burma and toward the northwest. Onions, chilli and tobacco are also grown here. The hill peoples cultivate many kinds of crops needed for their own consumption and for sale on a small scale because the terrain makes agriculture possible only on a limited scale.

Agriculture involves several types of cultivation. *Lai* cultivation is carried out in the Irrawaddy delta and its banks, Sittang valley, Arakan and Tenasserim which have regularly flooded fields during the rains. Paddy, which is rice before milling, is grown in these areas. *Kaing* cultivation is practiced along rivers and streams that have sand bar islands and sand banks during the dry season. Beans, peas, and vegetables are cultivated here. *Ya* cultivation is shifting cultivation practiced in the dry areas while *taung-ya* is slash-and-burn agriculture practiced by hill peoples.

Jade is smuggled from Burma into Chiang Mai, Thailand, as are antiques and other precious resources, in exchange for manufactured goods which are in short supply in Burma.

OTHER OCCUPATIONS

Apart from agriculture, Burmese are engaged in trading, manufacturing and services. Such occupations are found mainly in the urban centers. According to the 1983 census, 18% of the labor force were in wholesale and retail trade, 12.5% in manufacturing, 4.2% in services, and the rest in other sectors such as mining, construction, transport and communications. In terms of the gross domestic product (GDP in 1986/87) the shares of agriculture, manufacturing, mining, and trade, services and other were 40.3%, 9.3%, 0.9% and 50% respectively.

INFORMAL TRADE

The informal trade sector or the "black market" has been a large part of the economy since the years of socialism. Black marketeering is a result of severe economic deprivation in terms of a lack of local consumer items and the poor quality of locally-made items. Goods have been flowing in from Burma's neighboring countries in exchange for Burma's precious resources such as forest products, livestock, gems and minerals, agricultural products and antiques. These were exchanged for common plastic household items, medicine, clothing and textiles, and food and beverages. With the opening of the economy, it is expected that informal trade will decline, thus bringing legitimate earnings into the country's coffers.

INDUSTRIES

The first modern factories in Burma, set up during the reign of the last two kings in the 19th century, were glass and steel factories, and a mint.

During the British colonial period many industries such as rice milling and petroleum refining flourished but these were destroyed during the Second World War. After the war and after independence in 1948, industries were again established by many private entrepreneurs and by the government. Private entrepreneurs were active in the textile, food and beverages and chemical industries while the government was involved in pharmaceuticals, and cotton, jute and steel milling. However, private industries were nationalized by the government during the 1960s. Only very small private factories were left alone. In 1977, the Private Industries Law was passed; under this law some industries were opened to private entrepreneurs, including food, beverages and clothing.

The industrial policy of the socialist government was one of self-reliance and efforts were made to establish industries which could substitute for foreign imports. Large industrial complexes have been built such as those on the western bank of the Irrawaddy opposite Prome (Pyi) about 180 miles north of Rangoon; the complex in Syriam south of Rangoon; and Daik-u north of Rangoon. Cooperatives also participate in industrial production. However, because of lack of expertise and poor management and organization, these cooperatives have not been too successful in their ventures.

Garment-making is one industry which is open to private entrepreneurs.

Ships on the Irrawaddy. Burmese factories manufacture goods mainly for local consumption— Burma's major export items are primary products including rice and teak.

PRIVATE SECTOR VERSUS PUBLIC SECTOR

Food and beverages account for about 74% of the total manufacturing and processing output; the bulk is produced by privately-owned factories. Cloth and garments account for 5.1%. Other products such as construction materials, personal goods, industrial raw materials, mineral and petroleum products, and transport vehicles are 3.7%, 1.5%, 5.5%, 3.3%, and 1.9% respectively.

In terms of number of workers, private establishments with fewer than 10 workers numbered nearly 38,000 in 1989. At the other end of the scale, establishments with over 100 workers are mainly government-owned as shown in the following table.

The present military government has announced that it is no longer pursuing a socialist path but opening the country and inviting foreign investments. The government sectors are expected to be slowly reduced and the private sector allowed to enter many fields previously monopolized by the state.

FACTORIES AND ESTABLISHMENTS
(by number of workers, 1988/89)

No. of workers	State	Cooperative	Private	Total
Below 10 workers	981	409	37,965	39,355
10–50 workers	297	308	1,824	2,429
51–100 workers	150	–	9	159
Over 100 workers	426	–	4	430
Total	1,854	717	39,802	42,373

SOURCES OF REVENUE

Burma's revenue comes from the export of primary products and the country's main revenue has always been from the export of rice and rice products. During the British colonial period, Burma was the largest exporter of rice in the world, exporting an average of 3.3 million tons of rice annually. At present, however, Burma exports only about 0.5 million tons annually; the economic, social and political problems of the past two decades caused the decline in production. Nonetheless rice export earnings make up about 40% of total export earnings.

Besides rice, another major source of revenue is the export of teak and hardwoods, making up about 30% of total export earnings. Burma produces about 90% of the world's genuine teak and is believed to have at least three quarters of the total world reserves.

Rubber, jute, maize, beans and pulses are also major export items, as are metals and minerals such as zinc, tin and copper.

Burma is also famous for gems such as jade, rubies, sapphires and cultivated pearls, which are sold every year at the Gems Emporium to foreign gem merchants.

Export earnings in 1988 were about US$330 million.

Cultivated pearls are among the many gems sold every year at the Gems Emporium to foreign gem merchants.

WORK ETHIC

Traditionally, employers should look after their employees as a father does his children while employees should be loyal, faithful and honest. Buddhist teaching stresses the learning of a craft or skill early in life as one of the necessary ingredients for success, others being having good friends, spending modestly and guarding possessions already acquired.

Ingenuity is probably the main characteristic of Burmese at work. Burma is full of examples of this: 50-year old buses still run, as do old cars; many machines are run with locally-made parts produced from lathe machines. The isolation of the country for more than 25 years has served to reinforce this inborn trait.

Recycling was in existence in Burma long before the concept became popular in the west: old newspapers, books, magazines and exercise books have a ready market. Young children scrounge near garbage piles looking for scraps of plastic which can be resold to be melted down and remade into new plastic bags. Old plastic buckets, basins and baskets can similarly be melted and molded. Used oil drums can be used for storing water or rice. In households, old bottles and tins are always saved to store sugar, salt, flour and other kitchen ingredients. Car tires become rubber slippers.

Many private entrepreneurs have learned their business from family enterprises or when working as apprentices in other companies. They apply what they have learned and make ingenious adaptations rather than actual innovations. They are resourceful in spite of the restrictive conditions which the private sector faces.

Public servants, on the other hand, have very few incentives to work hard since promotion is by seniority or total number of years worked. They may indulge in moonlighting or do some petty trading, sell food and clothing, or lend money at interest—if they have sufficient capital—in order to stretch an arbitrarily low wage. Many also turn to petty bribery; people who want quick attention from public departments have to put up with this evil. At the very least, a favor is expected to be returned with another favor, and many departments work on this principle.

A small family-owned cheroot-making factory.

PEOPLE OF BURMA

SOCIAL HIERARCHY

NEXT TO the Buddhist monks, the aged receive the most respect. A Burmese family, however impoverished, would do its best to care for elderly, handicapped or sick relatives, even those quite distantly related. Homes for the aged are homes for those who have no one to care for them.

Being educated is worthy of great respect, no matter whether one has gainful employment or not. Proud parents of university graduates line living room walls with photos of their offspring in their graduation caps and gowns. A foreign degree is generally regarded as superior to local degrees and diplomas.

Among the professions, doctors and teachers are accorded high esteem. Doctors who practice for monetary fees alone are abhorred; they should be accommodating enough to accept their fees in kind, like bags of rice or cans of cooking oil. Relatives and close friends are "looked after" free of charge by most doctors.

The wealthy are looked up to, the more so if they do their share to help the needy. But it is all right for a person to be poor as long as he tries to live a morally upright and honest life.

At the bottom of the hierarchy are those who live on the fringes of society—beggars, lepers, cemetery dwellers. Most of these are taken care of by government welfare and health institutions, but a few remain outside the network.

Above: **A beggar is at the bottom of the social hierarchy.**

Opposite: **Buddhist monks receive the greatest honor from the Burmese. Very old monks who have lived austere and virtuous lives of spiritual rigor are especially venerated. Generally, however, it is the order of monks as a body, or the Sangha, rather than each individual monk, that is honored.**

ETHNIC GROUPS

The people of Burma are composed of a great many diverse people who first came into what is now known as Burma in three separate migrations

A Karen family.

from Central Asia and Tibet. The first migration brought the Mons and the Khmers. The second group of migrants was the Tibeto-Burmans, and the third, sometime in the 13th and 14th centuries, consisted of Tai-Chinese peoples.

Burmans, or ethnic Burmese, are the largest ethnic group, forming 69% of 38.6 million Burmese in 1987. Referred to generally as Burmese, as opposed to the other ethnic groups, they are descendants of the Burmans, Mons and the Tai-Chinese; typically they are dark and tall. Predominantly Buddhists, they live mostly in the river valleys and plains. Closely related to the Burmese are the Mons and Arakanese (Rakhine), who are also Buddhists, and mainly farmers.

Karens are second largest ethnic group; Sgaw and Pwo Karens are the two main Karen groups. They live in the Irrawaddy Delta and also in hilly Karen State. They form about 6.2% of the population.

The Shans, light-skinned and tall, are related to the Thais and the people of Laos, Cambodia and Vietnam. Mainly farmers, they live in the river valleys and lowland pockets of the Shan plateau.

The Chin people live in Chin and Arakan (Rakhine) States. About 30% of the Chin have converted to Buddhism and Christianity; the rest are animists, that is, they worship spirits.

Kachins live in Kachin State in the northernmost part of Burma. They are well known for their fierce fighting spirit, as are the Chin people. Kayah people were once known as Red Karen (Karenni) and live in Kayah State south of Shan State.

Apart from these main groups there are many other smaller ethnic groups such as Palaung, Padaung, Lisu, Wa, Danu, Lahu, Lashi, Yaw and others.

PADAUNG "GIRAFFE" WOMEN

A Burmese lady had just arrived on a visit to London. As she unpacked, her landlady stood near by and kept looking at the articles being unpacked. Finally unable to restrain herself, she asked the visitor, "Where are your neck rings?" This landlady's misconception was probably due to posters of Burma showing a Padaung woman with many copper rings about her neck. Actually the Padaung tribe numbers only a few thousand and are seldom seen in the lowlands, living in and around Loikaw, the Kayah State capital in east Burma. The rings are put on at an early age and increased year by year to a final total of about 20 lbs! This custom is said to be a deliberate deformation of the female tribe members to prevent them from being taken by other tribes. The rings depress the collar bones and ribs and make the neck look unnaturally long. In fact the rings cannot be removed without substituting a neckbrace as the neck is weakened, and there is a danger of suffocation otherwise!

DRESS

In place of trousers and skirts, Burmese men and women both wear a sarong called *longyi*, but tie it differently; men knot it in front and women fold it to the side. The men wear a shirt, with a small stiff collar, tucked into the *longyi*. A jacket is worn over the shirt for formal occasions. Women wear a waistlength blouse with an overlapping flap in front, over the *longyi*. For weddings and important functions they wear a shawl of netting over the blouse.

The *longyi* worn by the men is usually checked or striped while the women wear *longyi* with more varied designs: they may be handwoven with traditional motifs or in single colors, or they may be made from imported materials in *batik* or floral prints. For formal occasions silk *longyi* are essential for both men and women. Lace and brocade *longyi* are also worn by the women in the towns.

Younger girls nowadays prefer to wear western-type blouses or shirts, with a *longyi* worn calflength, which is short to Burmese eyes! Western dresses and skirts are also worn, but this is mainly in the capital city of Rangoon. Shorts, very skimpy blouses and miniskirts are not approved of, generally speaking: the exposure of too much skin is considered indecent. For visits to monasteries and pagodas Burmese women take care to wear long sleeves and thicker materials.

Men sometimes wear headgear called *gaung baung*, a close-fitting, brimless, silk hat with a loose piece at one side.

For the Burmese, footwear consists of a pair of thonged slippers, ordinary leather for everyday wear and velvet for special occasions.

The Burmese still wear their traditional dress of shirt (men) or blouse (women) and *longyi*, or sarong.

THE VERSATILE *LONGYI*

The men's *longyi* has all too often been a subject of ridicule. Actually it serves many purposes: when crossing a stretch of water or climbing a tree a man can hitch it up, gather the front portion toward the back, between the legs, and tuck it in at the waist so it becomes knickerbockers. It can be used to wipe a sweaty face; small articles can be carried in the front knot; young children can sit on a father's *longyi* between his legs as in a hammock; best of all it can be loosened after a big meal, or to cool one's legs on warm days! Old worn *longyi* become rugs or cool sheets for babies to sleep on. Women can bathe with modesty at the riverside or village well by drawing their *longyi* up and wrapping it around the upper part of the body. The *longyi* keeps one's legs warm and free of mosquitoes, and sitting cross-legged is easiest in a *longyi*.

Above: **The Shan bag is a flat woven strip of cloth folded in two with a strap attached and is carried from the shoulder (the Kachins use a similar bag). Colorful patterns are woven into the fabric which may be of wool, cotton, silk or artificial fibers. Schoolchildren use it for carrying books and pencil boxes to school, as do university students. It is giving way to sling bags and attaché cases, but remains a convenient means of carrying personal articles, and is easy on the shoulder. Sometimes it is slung across the chest, or the strap may be put over the forehead and the bag slung on the back.**

DRESS OF THE ETHNIC GROUPS While Mon and Arakanese peoples dress the same way as the majority of the Burmese, the other ethnic peoples of Burma wear many different costumes. Karens wear a woven striped tunic over trousers or *longyi*, and a scarf is tied around the head. Shan men wear loose black trousers tied as a men's *longyi*, with a shirt, while the women wear a longsleeved, tight, hip-length jacket and a *longyi*, and also a headscarf. Kayah women wear a cape over their shoulders and a long sash. Kachin women wear thick woolen skirts, leggings and black blouses decorated with silver disks and tassels, and their men wear black trousers and shirt. Chin women wear a woven tunic and skirt with a long shawl over the shoulders. Palaung women wear blue jackets with red collars and skirts with bamboo hoops.

HAIR STYLES

The hair of men used to be kept long and coiled into a topknot; in the colonial period, men came to sport a short hair style called *bo-kay* ("English-style hair").

As for the women, their hair styles have varied from dynasty to dynasty. Generally, women are expected to have long hair after they reach adulthood, and keep their hair rolled into a bun or *chignon*. They love to wear flowers at the side of their buns, like a garland of jasmine or a rosebud. Fragrance is appreciated more than beauty, so the *thazin*, a delicate and tiny orchid, is highly prized for its haunting fragrance; brides will pay a large sum to wear them in their hair on their wedding day! Nowadays, young mothers, and even older women, have opted for short hair, much to the dismay of their mothers!

Men's hair used to be kept long and coiled into a topknot.

Women traditionally kept their long hair rolled into a bun or *chignon*, but nowadays many younger women opt for short hair.

THANAKA

Thanaka is a pale yellow paste applied to the face by Burmese women and girls. It is obtained by grinding a piece of the bark of a small tree (*Murraya paniculata*) on a circular grinding stone with a few drops of water. This paste gives a cooling effect and reduces oiliness. Old grannies love to apply from head to toe the large amount of *thanaka* prepared by granddaughters. Young girls working in the hot sun, transplanting rice seedlings by hand, apply thick layers to keep from getting too brown. Today it can also be bought in powder or lotion form.

LIFESTYLE

ATTITUDES

A YOUNG CHILD dies, the parents are grief-stricken but accept it as *karma*. A dishonest person gets cheated, a cruel person dies a gruesome death, this is the working of *karma*—reaping what one has sown. A Buddhist belief, deeply rooted in the Burmese, is that everything that happens to oneself, both good and bad, is due to past deeds in this and former lives. By the same token every devout Buddhist knows that any deed done in this life may affect his future rebirth. Burmese Buddhists are afraid of *wut-ly-te*, meaning evil deeds follow a person without fail, in this existence and others.

Above: **Life in the village is more carefree than in the city. Here, the people live off the rich land, where the forests yield wild vegetables and the creeks are full of fish.**

Opposite: **The Burmese have a unique ability to remain cheerful even during times of great hardship.**

Burmese are, however, cheerful, fun-loving, happy-go-lucky people who are modest and easily contented. They love a good joke and a tall tale, happily spending a social evening around a pot of tea exchanging stories and anecdotes. Villagers are more carefree in that they do not worry so much about where their next meal will come from, since they have the trees and shrubs, and creeks full of fish on which to subsist. In the towns, life is not as easy: there are housing problems, and essential consumer goods such as rice, soap, meat and cooking oil are expensive and not readily available.

Burmese hospitality is *ah-nar-mu* at work. No unexpected visitor from out of town is turned away even when the house is full; room is somehow made for the person rather than causing him the inconvenience of looking for alternative accommodation.

AH-NAR-HMU

Ah-nar-hmu or *ah-nar-de* is an important principle governing social relationships among the Burmese and in their relationships with foreigners. It can roughly be defined as a feeling of hesitation in case one may be imposing a burden on another. An elderly aunt suffers in silence rather than tell her relatives that she is ill because she does not want to cause them the trouble of taking her to the doctor. A friend has borrowed some money and still has not returned it but never will the lender say a word to ask for the borrowed money to be repaid.

Ah-nar-hmu results in white lies and beating about the bush, but all Burmese feel a reluctance to cause another trouble, loss of face or hurt feelings. Western people with their characteristic directness are frustrated when they are unable to get a definite answer to a question but this is mainly because a strong negative answer is always avoided by most Burmese. Actually they will, if given sufficient time, come up with a solution that is acceptable to both sides.

FAMILY

Family ties are strong among Burmese. Buddhist tenets of duties and responsibilities of parents and children are still closely followed. Parents expect obedience and children have a duty to look after parents in their old age. The act of publicly disowning a child because of an unapproved marriage is not uncommon.

In many Burmese families you will find grandparents, uncles, aunts, and cousins living under one roof. Privacy is minimal, all disagreements and quarrels are soon known, and there are always attempts at reconciliation on the part of the elders. Everyone is expected to help in his own way, either by contributing toward expenses or helping in cooking, washing and other chores, or playing the role of adviser.

Burmese are greatly supportive of relatives, and they include those close and distant, and even close neighbors, who are referred to as "relatives from the same block." Relatives from out of town will always put up with a family rather than go to a hotel. When there are no relatives to stay with, out-of-towners prefer to stay in a monastery (after requesting permission of the chief monk). In Burma, hotels are for foreigners!

In urban areas there are now many smaller families consisting of a couple, children and a maid. Such parents do not receive the help and advice of their own parents as in extended families; this sometimes leads to a lower quality of family life for all concerned.

An extended Burmese family. Life is rich in such a household and one can always count on the support of the family in times of crises.

BIRTH

Birth is an auspicious occasion in any family. To be without children is regarded as being pitiable.

Before birth the expectant mother is required to be careful in what she eats and does; here, science and superstition appear to be well mixed (see "Common Taboos" opposite).

In the villages, pregnant women work in the fields or in other industries up to the last days before birth. Village midwives or elderly womenfolk attend to the birth. During the last decades, government rural health centers and health assistants have been available and traditional midwives have been gradually retrained. In the towns, mothers can receive free prenatal and postnatal care.

Rural folk have large families as each child can later contribute his labor on the farm. There is no strong preference for boys over girls as the birth of girls does not put a heavy burden on the parents with respect to dowry at marriage. Both boys and girls are accepted as gifts of "jewel children," meaning they are precious to their parents. Girls are expected to look after parents while boys are likely to be "given away" to in-laws.

A child is a gift, precious to its parents.

It was once the tradition to bury the umbilical cord at birth and, to this day, birthplaces are referred to as "the place where the cord is buried." The mother receives special care during the first days after delivery to clean her system, heal wounds and make her strong again. Many callers come to see the new baby with gifts and good wishes.

The child's name is chosen within a year. A ceremony may be held where the child's hair is washed with a herbal shampoo, guests invited and the child's health, wealth and freedom (from danger) wished for.

COMMON PREGNANCY AND BIRTH TABOOS

The pregnant mother should not eat—
    bananas or baby will be too big for normal delivery;
    chilli or baby will have no hair;
    glutinous rice as this will make the placenta stick to the womb.
She should not attend weddings or funerals.
She should leave some things incomplete during preparation such as
    partially sewing baby clothes, leaving out the hems on the diapers.
After birth she should not wash her hair for about a month.
She should not eat bamboo shoots or mushrooms for some time.
She should not handle soap.

It is said that when a baby smiles, it is because, although jealous spirits taunt it by saying "Your mother is dead," the baby knows this is untrue as it feeds at its mother's breast daily. When a baby cries, it is because jealous spirits say "Your father is dead," and the baby, not yet knowing the father, believes them.

CHILDREN

Most Burmese children have a carefree childhood. Parents are indulgent toward children, giving them what they ask for if or when they can afford it. Parents and grandparents may spoil and excuse them for mischief with "they are only children!" Parents often continue to look on their children as children and not as adults even after they are married and have children of their own!

Children are taken to most places and events except funerals. They are given a lot of attention, admired, commented on and never ignored. They are seen and heard. Certainly parents seldom ask the children to go away while an adults-only dinner or conversation takes place, and in any case the children soon get bored and will run away to play by themselves. Obedience is about the one thing that is expected of children.

Children living in the villages climb trees, fish in the creeks or go hunting in the forest. The boys may help by tending the cows while they graze in the pasture, and collecting firewood; girls help their mothers in the house with domestic chores or looking after younger children. Children may go to the village monastery to learn basic Burmese reading and writing or go to a government school. Some often have to walk several miles for this purpose.

In the towns, children may be seen playing in the streets. They may fly kites, a very dangerous thing in city streets both for the children and the motorists. They run light errands for parents who run a business, buy snacks from street-side vendors, or just watch people going by. Most children in the towns go to school; some children may be needed by their parents in their businesses and so stop their schooling after primary education at about ten or eleven years of age.

Chinlone is a favorite street game for town children.

PUBERTY

At about twelve or thirteen years the girls are gradually segregated from the boys; no more running around climbing trees or following the boys. In dress they start to wear *longyi* (sarong) and *aingyi* (blouse); no more bare legs; this may be one reason why Burma has so few sportswomen. Girls are also expected to keep their hair longer although this custom is slowly dying out.

Girls are expected to behave more quietly when speaking, laughing and walking, that is, to behave with more decorum. Bathing at village wells or by the river is in the company of other girls. They are expected to help their mothers around the house, and, in rural Burma, their formal education generally stops here.

At puberty or sometimes earlier, young boys go through an initiation ceremony when they wear the yellow robes of a Buddhist novice for a short period at a monastery. This ceremony is held either for a single boy or a group of them, economy and convenience being taken into consideration.

During the initiation ceremony for Buddhist novices, the boys are dressed up and taken around the village or town on decorated ponies or open cars. They go to the monastery where guests and relatives are assembled. Monks are offered alms and guests are fed later. In a ceremony that follows the boys are accepted into monkhood by the presiding monk. Their heads are shaved and they put on monk's robes. They are required to stay a few days at the monastery, fasting and abstaining from entertainment. They are taught the scriptures and, sometimes, basic meditation is practiced.

Some young girls go through an ear-piercing ceremony at the same time as their brothers and boy cousins become novices, but this ceremony does not have the same religious significance as the initiation. At this ceremony a girl will put on court dress and have her ears pierced and earrings put on. Because of the great expense of feasting guests, this ceremony is seen much less frequently nowadays.

Boys and girls brought up in the towns continue their education until the tenth standard when there is a country-wide matriculation examination. They are about sixteen to eighteen years old at this time. On passing this examination, they are able to pursue a university degree; in which discipline depends on how well they have done in the examination. Only those with very good results can go to medical and engineering schools.

ROLE OF WOMEN

Women are regarded as inferior to men in the sense that they can never be ordained as monks or become Buddhas unless they are reborn as men. Women are not allowed to enter certain parts of religious buildings such as the middle platform at the Shwe Dagon. Socially, however, their status is equal to men and if they defer to men it is due to their own wish to give men the privilege of feeling superior!

Women in Burma have always played an active role in the economy, whether in business, running a small roadside stall or a cheroot factory, or working the land.

Men are believed to have *hpon*, or "holiness" which is believed to be diminished if they touch women's skirts and underwear and other "unclean" articles. A man cannot prosper if his *hpon* is diminished. Some families wash men's clothing separately from the women's and also iron them with separate irons. Many women do their best to adhere to this practice.

In the family it is mostly the women who take charge of the household finances. Usually the husband hands over his pay check to be used appropriately. Women also supplement the family income in many ways, such as running a small shop in front of the house, buying and selling various articles, setting up a small industry making fruit preserves or cheroot, or acting as lenders of money or brokers for the sale of jewelry. Doing business comes quite naturally for most Burmese women.

Certain professions are regarded by parents as suitable and proper for their daughters—professions such as teaching, accounting, and secretarial jobs. As doctors, most become pediatricians or gynecologists because of the cultural segregation of the sexes and the taboo on touching between the sexes. Many women have broken into the ranks of lawyers and politicians which were for a long time the preserve of men.

Nursing was once the profession entered by Christian girls who are born to a religious code of kindness towards others and selflessness. In recent years many Burmese women have entered this profession as it brings a good income and is meaningful. At a time when many with university degrees are unemployed, young girls in their late teens and early twenties are enrolling at the nursing school instead of going to university. Most parents, however, desire a university education for their daughters and a large proportion of university students are female.

After marriage a woman keeps her own name. She may live with her own parents or with her in-laws. Deference is expected toward in-laws as toward her own parents, but it is not necessary for her to be in physical attendance at all times. If there is a divorce, half of all property acquired after marriage and what she originally brought to the marriage is hers. She can also freely remarry, whether she is divorced or widowed.

Socially, women enjoy equal status with men: a large proportion of university graduates are women, and women in professional and non-manual jobs earn the same wage as men in the same grade of appointment.

MARRIAGE

Beginning from their teens, young girls and boys are generally segregated but they have many opportunities to meet at village activities, at school, in the university and at work as they grow into their twenties.

Courtship customs among the Burmese used to consist of writing love letters, initiated by the boy. In modern times the telephone has also been a means of communicating feelings. Dating usually takes place only when a girl has accepted a boy as a possible candidate for marriage. Groups of boys and girls may go out to tea shops or the movies.

A courting couple.

Arranged marriages are still found among Burmese. Parents hope for a person with roughly the same ethnic background, economic status and education for their child. A go-between, who is a relation of either party, helps.

Marriages based on mutual love are also common, but parental approval is desired and sought. Where parents cannot agree to the marriage, relatives try to help in achieving a reconciliation.

Before the Second World War and after independence, eligible males were mainly those in the civil service, doctors and engineers. This is still the case, but their ranks are now increased by merchant seamen who have ʼined social status due to their earning power in a deteriorating economic ʼation.

Engagements are not really necessary, but announcements can be made in the newspapers. A small ceremony may be held at the home of the bride-to-be with parents of both parties and relatives present. The qualifications and virtues of the bridegroom-to-be will be extolled by an elder who knows him well, similarly for the bride-to-be. Rings may be exchanged.

Marriage in Burma involves only the mutual consent of the two parties concerned. Living and eating together is enough to constitute marriage. Traditionally the marriage is valid if neighbors recognize it as such.

Weddings can be as simple or elaborate as the parents and the couple wish. The simplest wedding is that held before a gathering of elders in the bride's home, the bride and groom sitting together on a smooth mat paying obeisance to the Triple Gems (see page 67) and parents. Monks may be invited and offered alms. Others simply go to the court and sign a marriage contract before witnesses, and a lawyer or judge.

The most elaborate weddings are held in Rangoon's hotels, where several hundred guests are invited. They are entertained by a music troupe and well known singers before the bride and groom are married in the presence of the guests. The marriage ceremony is performed by a master of ceremonies dressed like a Brahmin. The hands of bride and groom are tied with a silk scarf and dipped in silver bowl of water. Conch shells are blown, and silver coins a confetti are scattered over the guests. Refreshments are served aft ceremony, usually tea with cakes, sandwiches and ice cream.

Newly-weds usually stay with the bride's parents for a short while before into their own

DEATH

To the Burmese, death is just one stage in the life cycle and is accepted. The dead person is simply leaving his body behind to move on to a new rebirth in the endless cycle of existence. The family grieves but not for a long period of time. No mourning periods are specified by the religion.

When a person dies away from his residence, for example on the way to the hospital, the body is not allowed back into the village or street quarter. It is usual to see just outside the village boundary a corpse in its coffin laid out for burial.

The funeral of a young girl outside the village. The coffin is decorated thus to ward off ghosts and spirits.

On the day a person passes away the family brings in a monk and makes an offer of food to the family's monastery to indicate that a life has been lost. The dead person is bathed and dressed in his or her favorite clothes. Candles, incense sticks, water and token offerings of food are placed at the head. An earthen water pot is placed under the bed on which the body is laid.

The spirit of the dead is believed to be still in and near the residence up to a week after death. There is a wake which lasts a whole week. Doors and windows are kept open throughout this period. In villages, all the villagers help. The youth help by staying awake through the night and letting the family members, exhausted by grief and by talking to callers the whole day, take a rest. They stay awake by playing cards, drinking plain tea and eating snacks. Other neighbors help to cook the food for the family and other helpers.

A week later, monks are invited again to be given alms, to pray and to remind the spirit of the deceased that he is no longer a member of the household and must go on his own way. All merits are shared with him in order that he might be reborn to a better life.

At the funeral, the height of each member of the family is measured with thread; the lengths of thread are then put into the coffin. A 25-*pya* coin (US$0.04) is placed in the mouth of the deceased to be used as payment to the ferryman when crossing to the land of the dead. The water pot is broken. For the bereaved their grief reaches a climax and there is no restraint in weeping and exclaiming; it is believed that the relief of crying is healthy for the bereaved. Burial is usual in Burma but in Rangoon, the capital, cremation is common.

Among the ethnic groups, the Buddhist Karens living in the Karen State perform a bone collection ceremony a year after death. The bones of the dead are collected and placed in a special hut and food and prayers are offered.

In the villages very simple markers are used for the graves and there is generally no effort to maintain graves or a day such as All Souls' Day. Instead the dead are remembered at feasts offered to monks for the purpose of sharing merit with them. Many other good deeds may be done by the remaining members of the family to help the dead on their way along the cycle of existence, such as donations to homes for the aged, donating scripture books, building monasteries and so on.

The *pyattaik*, or celestial chariot, bears the body of a priest, on the third day of the funeral, to the top of a high hill from where he ascends to heaven from a pyre of fragrant sandalwood, accompanied by fireworks.

RELIGION

BUDDHISM

ABOUT 85% of Burma's population is Buddhist; this includes about 99% of the Burmese, Shans and Karens. The Buddhism practiced in Burma is Theravada Buddhism, similar to that found in Thailand, Laos, Sri Lanka and Cambodia (Kampuchea) and different from the Mahayana Buddhism of China, Japan, Korea, Tibet, Nepal and Vietnam.

The Buddha was not a god but a human being, a prince of a kingdom in India who lived more than 2,500 years ago, about 623 years before Christ. He renounced the world at the age of twenty-nine to look for a cure for the ills of the world, including disease, old age and death. He practiced all forms of austerity for a period of six years, but it was through meditation that he gained Omniscience, or Enlightenment, having understood the Four Noble Truths and found the Middle Way, or Eightfold Path, a guideline to escape from the sufferings of all mankind.

Above: **The Buddha preaching the Four Noble Truths at the very first sermon after his Enlightenment.**

Opposite: **Buddhism strongly influences life in Burma. Daily at the temples and pagodas, one finds many devotees sitting in prayer or quiet meditation.**

THE FOUR NOBLE TRUTHS

The Four Noble Truths discerned by the Buddha on reaching Enlightenment are, first, that all life involves pain, suffering, birth, disease, old age and death. No matter how wealthy one may be one cannot escape any of these ills. Second, the reason for these ills is craving, desire or attachment to things, pleasures and people. Third, detachment can bring an end to pain and an escape from the cycle of rebirths. Fourth, detachment can be achieved by following the Eightfold Path.

The Tripitaka, or Three Baskets, is the Buddhist scripture.

BUDDHIST PHILOSOPHY   The basic philosophy of Buddhism is that the universe and all forms of life in it are in a constant process of change, from birth to death. After death, there is rebirth; the endless cycle of death and rebirth is known as the Wheel of Rebirth. There are 31 planes of existences into which a being can be born depending on his *karma*, which is the result of his thoughts, deeds and speech. Some of these planes of existence are the animal plane, the ghost planes, the human plane and the celestial planes.

The law of *karma* is a law of cause and effect: whatever happens to one is the result of one's past actions—including thought, deeds and speech—in previous existences, and one can expect to reap the result of one's actions in this existence in future lives. The ideal goal of a Buddhist should be to reach *nirvana* and make a complete break from the cycle of existences. *Nirvana* is defined as an extinction of greed, anger and delusion (belief in ego or self). The way to reach *nirvana* is to acquire morality, concentration and wisdom, or insight, by following the Eightfold Path.

THE EIGHTFOLD PATH

The Eightfold Path consists of Right Understanding, Right Thought (grouped as wisdom), Right Speech, Right Action, Right Livelihood (grouped as morality), Right Effort, Right Mindfulness, and Right Concentration (grouped as concentration). There are strict definitions of what constitutes "Right;" right speech, for example, means refraining from empty chatter, tale-telling and abuse.

BUDDHIST WORSHIP   The Buddhists worship the Triple Gems which are the Buddha, the Dhamma, or his teaching, and the Sangha, or his disciples, the monks. The Dhamma, which means "truth" or "law," consists of the scriptures known as the Tripitaka (Three Baskets). The Buddhist cannot beseech the Buddha for fulfillment of wishes. He does all he can to gain merit by keeping the five rules of abstaining from killing any living beings, stealing, adultery, lying, and taking intoxicants, and occasionally, the eight rules which include celibacy, avoiding entertainment and adornment, and avoiding sleeping on luxurious beds. These are only the fulfillment of morality. For wisdom and concentration he has to practice meditation in any one of 42 methods.

OTHER FAITHS

Buddhists form the majority of the population but there are Christians, Hindus, Moslems, Chinese Taoists, Confucians, Jews and animists.

The earliest conversions to Christianity took place around the early 17th century. A significant number of Karens, Chin, Kachin and Burmese are Baptists. Christian missionaries were active from the colonial period up to the mid-1960s, establishing schools, and running hospitals and social welfare centers. After 1962 these establishments were nationalized by the government.

The Sangha is the order of monks whose role is to spread the teaching of the Buddha, give guidance in meditation methods and to confirm the laymen's belief or confidence in the Buddha and the Dhamma. Monks enter the order at any age and can remain as long as they wish. They follow a strict set of 227 rules of conduct, keep 10 rules which include no food after noon, no entertainment, and celibacy. They are forbidden to practice skills—such as medicine and astrology—that may be wrongly used to gain followers or donations.

Right: **Pagodas have eight posts at the eight compass points, for each day of the week plus an extra day created by dividing Wednesday into two days. Each day is characterized by an animal. To Burmese the day of the week on which one is born is as important as one's birth date.**

Below: **A household shrine.**

PLACES OF WORSHIP

To a visitor, every hilltop in Burma appears to have a pagoda on the summit, even if they are small and only whitewashed. Burma has often been called the Land of Pagodas. Trekkers to Mt. Victoria, Burma's third highest peak, have often reported a cheated feeling to find a pagoda on reaching the top (10,000 feet)! Pagodas are usually built on heights since they contain holy relics and should never be on a level lower than people's houses.

Pagodas are solid conical structures with a central treasure vault below. A terrace around the pagoda provides pilgrims with space for praying, meditating, telling beads or making offerings. Temples are built with a hollow chamber in the center, unlike pagodas, and pilgrims can enter the temple. Other Buddhist structures include Buddha images built in the open or under a shelter. A Dhamma-yone is a place where sermons and feasts are held.

Entrances to large pagodas and temples are lined with small stalls selling flowers and sprigs of leaves, candles, gold leaf, small paper umbrellas, streamers and fans to be offered to the Buddha. It is the custom to remove shoes and slippers on entering these places. Burmese women mainly take a brown shawl or scarf which is wrapped around from one shoulder across to the waist when praying.

Monasteries are places where monks reside but people may also go there to pay their respects and offer alms of food and provisions, money, and robes. They may spend a whole day or several days at a monastery observing the rules and meditating in one of the *zayat* (resting places) in the grounds. Many religious feasts, including those for initiation and robe-offering ceremonies, are held in monasteries. Women are forbidden to enter some parts of a monastery.

This church, in the hill station of Maymyo, was built by the British.

Every Buddhist household has a shrine in the living room, either built into a wall or placed on a high table or cupboard. Images of the Buddha, some of which may have belonged to ancestors, are placed together with images of Buddha's disciples, and pictures of famous pagodas, monks and relics. Flowers, candles, water and food are offered daily.

In Burma, faiths other than Buddhism are also freely worshiped and one can find churches, cathedrals, mosques, Hindu temples and Chinese temples in Rangoon and many other towns in the country.

HOLY SYMBOLS AND RELIGIOUS RITES

Burmese Buddhists show reverence to the Buddha by keeping the Buddha's image in their household shrine and offering flowers, candles, water and food. The food is a token portion from a newly cooked pot of rice, a new cake, or fruit just bought and washed. It is offered at dawn or early morning and thrown away at noon. Flowers are changed as they wither, and water changed daily. The Buddha's image is a visual aid which reminds the Buddhist that the Buddha really lived over 2,500 years ago and was a Supreme human being, and confirms his confidence or belief in the teaching of the Buddha.

Banyan trees are seldom cut down; instead, small *nat* (spirit) shrines are built on or near them.

Buddhists hold their palms together in reverence when they pass a pagoda or meet monks. Pagodas are sacred because most of them contain relics of the Buddha inside their central vault. Books and pictures of the Buddha are also sacred and these should never be placed underfoot or stepped over. Certainly Buddha images should never be lower than head level! It pains Buddhists to see images of the Buddha placed at the foot of stairs as decoration, inside bookshelves, and even used as umbrella and hat stands.

The banyan tree is holy because it is the tree under which the Buddha reached Enlightenment; banyan trees are seldom cut down. Small shrines are built on their trunks and flowers and candles are offered. Drooping branches of the banyan are sometimes propped up with bamboo poles as a merit for a sick or dying person.

When misfortunes come to a family, it is usual to invite monks to the home, offer them alms, and request them to recite the *paritta* or scriptures which are believed to have the power to overcome dangers, disease and misfortunes. Flowers, water in a bowl, sand and spools of thread are placed before the monks. After the recitation, the water is drunk as holy water, sand sprinkled around the house, the thread cut up whenever necessary and tied around the house or around wrists of children.

After prayers, a devotee beats a small triangular gong with a small wooden mallet, or rings a bell, as a symbol of sharing merit with all beings. Golden umbrellas are placed on hearses of those who have built pagodas and monasteries in their lifetime.

A 24-petaled chrysanthemum is used as a symbol of the Paticcasamupada, the Law of Dependent Origination, which explains the cyclic chain of rebirth from which one is unable to escape. It sometimes symbolizes Pathana, the 24 Causes.

Above: **A 24-petaled chrysanthemum is used as a symbol of the Law of Dependent Origination, the cyclic chain in which beings are reborn again and again, and from which they are unable to escape.**

Left: **After prayers, a devotee strikes a small triangular gong as a symbol of sharing merit with all beings.**

71

FOLK BELIEFS

In spite of centuries of Buddhist practice, animism, the worship of spirits, which has existed from an even more remote time, continues to exist side by side with Buddhism. Ghosts and demons have not been seen by many but that is no reason not to believe those who have!

At a festival, an offering of bananas, rolled tobacco leaves and other foods is made to the *nat*.

The Burmese spirit world has thirty-seven *nat*, or spirits. Most of these are spirits of those who have died a violent death. Shrines are built for them and offerings made. Most of these spirits are appeased out of fear for they are capable of punishing more than rewarding, but that does not mean that one cannot ask for health, fame or fortune!

Even among those who have given up animistic worship, a spell of bad luck and a visit to an astrologer can make them revert back to their traditional worship to appease spirits who still want their offerings.

For *nat* worship, it is the custom to hang a green coconut in a small basket in a corner of the living room. If there is an illness, for example, and the stem of the coconut is found to be dry, it is assumed that the spirit is angry because the coconut has not been replaced by a fresh one earlier. Those who work on the stage, make movies or play in orchestras customarily need to offer bananas, coconut and tobacco leaf to the spirit of the arts before performances.

Cursing for a person to die, even in jest, is frowned on; statements such as "Bye-bye, I'm going and not coming back again" and similar words are believed to be ill omens of death and bad luck. Children are admired, but one should never say how fat, how heavy or how healthy they are in case the spirits get jealous and make them sick. Nor should one say "I never get sick, never catch a cold." Wives should not wash their hair when their husbands are away. Hair should not be washed or cut on Monday, Friday or the day of one's birth. Hair should not be washed in the evening and let down loose after dark. Pots should not be banged with ladles as this may invite hungry ghosts. Clothes should not be put on backwards in play (corpses are dressed this way). Children should not hide inside rolls of mats.

Woodcutters and hunters who live off the jungle are very careful with their language so as not to anger forest spirits. Fishermen and miners have their own spirits to worship. Some places are believed to have particularly powerful spirits and visitors are warned not to anger them by making jokes, or belittling them as they can make one lose one's way, and make other trouble. One should never say "come along everyone" when passing cemeteries, as ghosts may follow one.

People relieving themselves under trees and bushes may mentally ask for forgiveness from any spirits that are believed to be living in these places.

One should not have a haircut on Monday, Friday or the day of one's birth.

MAGIC

Black magic or sorcery is widely practiced, especially in villages. Villagers may be afraid of someone who seems to possess some magical powers. Spells may be cast on children and adults, sometimes not out of malice or anger but love! These spells can be reversed by those who have the power to undo the spell and punish the perpetrator. These people are not monks but lead virtuous lives in order to possess the power to drive away evil spirits. They give charms such as holy thread and holy water, or make offerings to prevent or break a spell. A spell may manifest itself in illness or strange behavior that cannot be cured by conventional medicine. If a person dies and a spell is suspected it is usual to cremate the body; the spell is said to remain unburned in the ashes and can be removed.

Spells may be hidden in food, which is then fed to unsuspecting victims, or they may be buried in the victim's garden or under his house. These spells, called *inn*, are pieces of slate, wood, bone or foil on which squares are made and filled in with letters or numbers. The very same kind of *inn*, but "good" ones, are dispensed by astrologers to deflect any bad luck. The squares are placed on altars, and lighted candles placed on them.

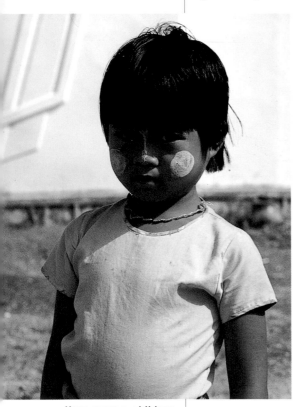

Very young children wear holy thread around their necks or wrists to protect them.

Besides "magicians," clairvoyants, astrologers and palmists abound in Burma. They are consulted by those who wish for certainty at some point of their lives. When a clairvoyant's powers become known people line up at the doorstep.

Astrologers are consulted to pick auspicious days for weddings or ground-breaking ceremonies, or when there is illness or general failure in life. To change the luck of a person, an astrologer may offer a change of name, or advise offering certain flowers and leaves to the Buddha; or he may advise on the kind of merit one should make, for example, the number of birds and fishes to set free, the number of rounds of rosary to tell, or kinds of food to avoid. Astrologers and palmists may be found at roadsides and on pagoda grounds.

A roadside palm reader in Rangoon. Palmists and astrologers are consulted by those who wish for certainty at some point in their lives.

The majority of the population being Burmese, the most widely spoken language is Burmese.

LANGUAGE

SPOKEN LANGUAGE

BURMESE, the official language, belongs to the Tibeto-Burman language group. To a foreign ear Burmese sounds much like Chinese. It is monosyllabic and tonal; a failure to pitch correctly results in meaningless sentences.

Spoken Burmese differs from region to region, some regional accents being quite strong. In regions such as the eastern state of Arakan (Rakhine), and Tavoy and Mergui in the south, the dialects spoken are forms of old Burmese.

The young people in Burma speak slang, which is naturally frowned upon by the older people as being coarse, decadent and "hippie." However, it continues to be a popular medium of communication and its usage is reinforced by comic books, cartoons, novels and popular songs.

Having spent many years as a British colony, most Burmese can speak or at least understand simple English. Those Burmese who were of school age during the Japanese occupation of Burma are able to speak simple Japanese.

The ethnic groups speak their own languages. The Kachin, Chin and Karen each has a romanized alphabet developed by the early missionaries. The Shan and Mon also have their own writing. Most Burmese are unable to speak the ethnic languages while ethnic groups have learned to speak Burmese.

Ethnic groups, including the Akhas above, speak their own languages although they have learned to speak Burmese well.

FORMS OF ADDRESS

For the Burmese, how one addresses or speaks to a person depends on his or her age and social status. When addressing monks, a special form of speech must be used. Elders, teachers, doctors and those worthy of respect are addressed in polite form. Honorifics must be used with such persons, while among equals—in age or social status—a freer form of speech is used. "U" and "Daw" are used for addressing adult men and women respectively; "Ko" and "Maung" are used for younger men, and "Ma" for young women. "Saya" is used for teachers, doctors, or bosses, "sayama" being the feminine form.

FIRST ENGLISH-BURMESE DICTIONARY

The first English-Burmese dictionary was compiled by Adoniram Judson (1788–1850), an American Baptist missionary, during the middle of the 19th century. Judson had arrived in Burma in 1813. In 1824, during the second Anglo-Burmese war, he was imprisoned together with other foreigners, in the capital of Ava, and was released a year later.

Judson completed the English-Burmese dictionary in 1849 while the Burmese-English dictionary remained unfinished at the time of his death. It was completed only in 1852 by another missionary, E.O. Stevens. These two dictionaries are in use to this day.

OLD BURMESE MANUSCRIPTS

In the past Burmese wrote on paper, lacquered boards and palm leaves. A Burmese book of paper, or *parabaik*, may be eight feet long and eighteen inches wide, and folded like a concertina, each fold being about six inches long and eighteen inches wide. Palm leaf manuscripts, or *pay-sar*, are palm leaves trimmed, sewn, and folded like a concertina, and written on with a metal stylus. Religious, literary, and scientific works, letters, and horoscopes, were in the form of palm leaf manuscripts. Lacquer manuscripts, or *kammavaca*, contain Buddhist scriptures in Pali, written in a square script (see below).

BURMESE SCRIPT

The Burmese alphabet consists of thirty-three letters, which are combined with various symbols to indicate the tones. The letters are circular in appearance. These letters were originally square, derived from rock-cut scripts of South India, but have gradually become rounded.

While the alphabet was derived from the Phalpava script of South India, it did not come directly from the original source. The Burmese obtained their alphabet from the Mons of ancient Thaton who had earlier received religious writings in Pali, possibly from the 5th century Buddhist center in Madras.

The Burmese alphabet.

BURMESE NAMES

To those used to a system of family names, Burmese names are very confusing because surnames are entirely unnecessary. At work there may be a number of persons having the same name, in which case it is perhaps more expedient to give them numbers! In one organization in Rangoon, there are about twenty U Maung Maung's. Most parents go by the Burmese name-choosing method where each day of the week is assigned the various letters of the alphabet, and parents choose a name beginning with any of the letters belonging to the day on which the child is born.

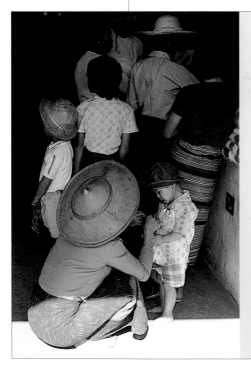

CHOOSING A NAME THE BURMESE WAY

Letters assigned to the different days of the week are:

Monday	– ka, kha, ga, nga
Tuesday	– sa, hsa, za, nya
Wednesday	– wa, la
Thursday	– pa, hpa, ba, ma
Friday	– tha, ha
Saturday	– ta, hta, da, na
Sunday	– a

U Ba Khin (Thursday born) and wife Daw Khin Khin (Monday born) might name their Friday born daughter Ma Thet Thet. Care has to be taken in picking the name as certain combinations of letters are supposed to be favorable and others bring bad luck to a person.

ASTROLOGY AND NAMES

Some parents name their child with the help of an astrologer who makes astrological calculations and chooses a name designed to lessen the bad aspects foreseen and to bring good fortune to the child.

It is also quite common for people to change their names in mid-life, on the advice of an astrologer, in order to change their luck for the better. In these circumstances the way to establish an identity is to ask who the parents are, where they come from or live and what work they do, and so on, until at one point one can place a person.

အမည်ဖြည့်စွက်ခြင်း

ဦးကြီးမြင့် (ခ) ဦးသူတော်၏ သား ဦးအောင်ဒင်အမျိုးသားမှတ်ပုံတင် အမှတ် LLM-006379 အား ယနေ့မှ စ၍ ဦးအောင်ဒင်(ခ)ဦးခင်စိုးဟုပြည့်စွက်ခေါ် ကြပါရန်။

An advertisement in the newspaper announcing a change of name. "U Aung Din, National Registration No. LLM 006379, son of U Kyi Myint (aka) U Thu Daw, will from today henceforth be known as U Aung Din (aka) U Khin Soe."

NICKNAMES

Nicknames are quite common especially in childhood. These nicknames are given in the spirit of love and humor; a very dark child might be called Maung Mai, or Master Blackie. Some nicknames are deliberately demeaning. Alternatively, a very sickly child may be called Maung Than Chaung, or Master Iron Bar, so that he may grow stronger and sturdier.

In many families the children are nicknamed by their position in the family such as Ko Ko (big brother), Ma Ma (elder sister), Nyi Nyi (younger brother) and Nyi Ma Lay (youngest sister).

NONVERBAL LANGUAGE

The Burmese are an informal people but they do consider it important that due respect be shown to elders and those of higher social status, not only in speech but also in posture. For example, when elders are on a mat it is not decent for a younger person to be sitting on a chair. Similarly, to pass objects over the heads of elders is disrespectful; when handing an object to an elder, the left hand is held at the right elbow to show respect.

The *kadawt* gesture is a way of honoring one's elders.

To talk to an elder who is sitting at a lower level, the younger party will slightly bow from his standing position. When passing in front of elders, respect is shown by walking past, bowing slightly. When passing pagodas, or meeting monks, one holds one's palms together as a gesture of reverence.

The Burmese show their respect for parents, grandparents, teachers, and those to whom gratitude is due with the *kadawt* gesture, a way of honoring and asking for forgiveness for any thoughtless acts. Kneeling, palms held together, they crouch down to the floor, touching the floor with forehead and elbows. This gesture, like a small ceremony, is made when younger people are going on a journey, or an elder is leaving, on some festival day, when a favor has been received from a superior, and when an elder passes away.

BURMESE SMILE

As with other Asian peoples the Burmese smile readily. A Burmese doctor studying in England would smile every time he met his Professor in passing. It was meant as a greeting but one day the Professor stopped him and asked, "Am I very funny?"

A smile may convey a greeting or a consent, or it may express an emotion like amusement, embarrassment, shyness, sarcasm or anger.

The head and hair of a person are held reverent and the lowliest parts of the body are the feet. A Burmese in his office will never put his feet even on his own desk, and to use the feet in pointing or kicking is very rude. Shoes and slippers have to be removed when entering Burmese homes, monasteries or pagodas.

Although women are accorded equal status to men, they are not allowed to enter certain places such as higher levels of pagodas. Their garments, especially their *longyi* (sarong), are never hung in front of the house or overhead.

Most Burmese are embarrassed by any show of affection in public and touching is generally taboo between the sexes even among members of a family. On the beach one will not see any young Burmese man with a lady taking a ride on his shoulders! At religious congregations the women are seated separately from the men.

ARTS

TRADITIONAL DRAMA

MANY BURMESE love to watch a classical drama known as *zat* which is based on the 550 *Jataka* tales told by the Buddha, in which he describes his past existences and encounters with relatives, disciples and enemies. In these tales, the Buddha's heroic deeds, wisdom and courage—before he had achieved enlightenment—are portrayed. The *zat* takes all night to perform, and is punctuated by dancing, and singing by the dancers themselves or by a backstage vocalist.

The *zat* is performed in a *zat-yone*, a large bamboo structure with a stage, or just an open-air area with a bamboo matting fence. The audience sits on mats which have to be brought. A family may bring about four to six mats if children, grandparents and others are included. They bring food, usually snacks such as *lepet* (pickled tea), which helps to keep them awake, beverages, cheroots, and *betel* for chewing. Very young babies are breast fed while mothers watch the play. Some of the audience doze off now and then so the play is probably watched in parts..

The *zat* starts only at about midnight and finishes at sunrise. In the earlier part of the evening there are short dances.

Another well known drama is the *yamazat*, a Burmese version of the Ramayana. It is performed by actors wearing masks, the principal characters being Princes Yama and Lekkhana (the brothers), Princess Thida, the ogre, and Hanuman, the monkey.

Above: **A village holds an all-night-long *zat* on the occasion of a pagoda festival. In the early evening, before the play begins, the audience is entertained by short dances.**

Opposite: **The *Jataka* tales, told by the Buddha about his existences before Enlightenment, are depicted here on a wall mural in the Lokahteikpan temple at Pagan.**

MARIONETTE THEATER

The marionette theater probably originated from the time of King Nga Sint Gu Min in the late 18th century, although there is some evidence that it existed during the Ava period (mid-17th century). The Minister for royal entertainment, U Thaw, is attributed as being its originator. Social relationships between the sexes were so restricted at that time that puppets substituting for real actors became very popular and the marionette theater flourished.

The Burmese marionette theater has all but disappeared with the emergence of other performing arts, and can only be seen at some pagoda festivals.

Burmese marionettes require great skill to manipulate, as some of them may have as many as sixty strings. Some puppets can even move their eyebrows! The marionette show has to have twenty-eight characters: a king, an old woman, a prince, a princess, two princes regent (one white-faced and the other red), one astrologer, one hermit, one *nat* (spirit), one *mahadeva* (deity), one old man, two buffoons, two worshipers, a horse, two elephants (one black and one white), a tiger, a monkey, two parrots, one dragon, a wizard, and four ministers. The puppet masters manipulate their puppets while female and male impersonators sing and recite the parts.

The marionette theater has almost vanished; the emergence of other performing arts takes away audiences and therefore performers, and when old puppet masters die there are no new masters to take their places. At present the marionette show is very rare and can be seen only at some pagoda festivals.

MODERN THEATER

The *pya-zat* (*pya* means "to show" and *zat* means "story") is a relatively modern musical stage-play with many songs and a simple plot. Unlike a western musical, however, there is usually no dancing. Speech is in simple prose whereas in traditional drama parts are spoken in verse and recited. The *pya-zat* started as a mime known as "live bio-scope" because it imitated the silent movies but involved live actors. It was popular before the Second World War and after independence but slowly disappeared after the 1950s with the increasing popularity of the movie theater.

The late appearance of this type of play, in the 1930s, has been attributed to the social taboos during the last dynasty, the Konbaung period which, among other things, forbade a man and woman to be seen together unless they were man and wife.

In 1943, a number of theater halls were built in Rangoon. The plays were performed on stage and orchestras played below the stage. Between 1943 and 1969 over 200 plays were staged, of which about 180 were musical plays. These *pya-zat* are now being revived by the present government, and play to full houses.

An open-air movie theater to which Burmese throng when night falls. The increasing popularity of the movie theater after the 1950s led to the decline of the *pya-zat*, or musical stage-play.

The marionette theater has influenced this Burmese dance in which dancers in resplendent court dress move like puppets.

DANCE

Burmese dance has existed from pre-Buddhist times when *nat* worship was performed with dance. Burmese dance is rather vigorous and requires some difficult acrobatic feats. It is also quite decorous and male and female dancers do not touch when dancing together. Young beginners are taught the *ka-bya-lut*, a basic traditional dance.

An interesting dance is one in which dancers perform like puppets. It has been said that Burmese dance had to be copied from puppets because the marionette theater had replaced human dancers for a period. The principal female dancer wears a court dress with a bodice and long-sleeved jacket which has stiff curved edges at the hips; the *longyi* has a train which the dancer kicks out as she dances. Principal male dancers dress as princes in silk *longyi*, jacket and white headdress. Other roles include pages, soldiers, *zawgyi* (wizard) and *nat*.

The *yein*, a popular dance at Water Festival celebrations, involves uniformly dressed dancers, usually female, dancing in unison, while a *hna-par-thwa* is a duet. The elephant dance, performed at the Elephant Dance Festival in Kyaukse near Mandalay, has the dancers in a papier-mâché and bamboo frame elephant costume.

The *anyein* is a combination of solo dancing and clowning by *lu-pyet*, or clowns, who make jokes about current events, and various other topics, some of which are quite bawdy. During the intervals when the clowns appear, the dancer rests or changes her costume. Sometimes two or more dancers take turns in dancing. The entire performance lasts about two hours.

Many of the ethnic dances are performed with swords or different kinds of drums. Ethnic dances include group dancing in which young boys and girls dance together, which is not very common in Burmese dance.

The elephant dance is performed at the Elephant Dance Festival in Kyaukse near Mandalay, but also may be seen at a village festival.

MUSIC

Burmese music has been described by westerners as being disconcerting with its various separate strains from drums, gongs, cymbals, bamboo clappers, flute and oboe. The sounds are in sharp contrast rather than in harmony.

A Burmese orchestra performing at a pagoda festival.

When the Burmese king Hsinbyushin invaded and conquered Siam in the 18th century, many Siamese musicians, dancers, composers and craftsmen were brought to Burma, and Burmese culture and music have been greatly influenced by this augmentation. A type of classical song and dance is known as *yodaya,* meaning Siamese. Western musical instruments such as violin, piano, mandolin, guitar and accordion have also been incorporated into Burmese music.

The Burmese orchestra consists of a drum circle, gong circle, bamboo clappers, wind instruments including *hne*—which has a high-pitched sound—and flute, and cymbals. Apart from the drum circle, there is also a large drum, hung from an ornamental winged dragon. The drum and gong circles are bright and colorful, decorated with glass mosaic and gold paint; they can be taken apart during transportation and reassembled at the performance venue. There are twenty-one drums in a large drum circle, nine in a small drum circle. A gong circle has nineteen gongs. Sometimes, instead of a gong circle, there is a gong rectangle which consists of a row of gongs hung from a rectangular frame, and has fewer gongs than a gong circle.

For celebrations different kinds of drums are used. The *sidaw* (large drum) is for important formal occasions, the *ozi* (pot-shaped drum) and *dobat* (two-faced drum) are for village celebrations, and the *bonshay* (long drum) and *bongyi* (big drum) are for plowing and harvesting festivals. A Burmese drum is tuned with a piece of dough, of boiled rice and wood ash, which is stuck to its base, and determines its tone. A melody can be played on the drum circle as the drums have different tones.

The *saung-gauk* Burmese harp is a 13-stringed instrument shaped like a boat. The harpist sits and holds the harp in the lap when playing. Classical songs are accompanied by the harp. The *puttalar* xylophone is made of bamboo or wooden pieces.

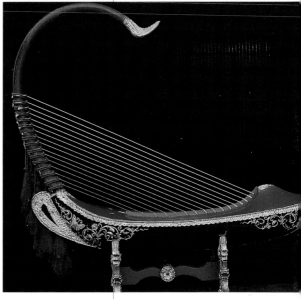

Burmese harp

Ethnic musical instruments are many and varied in shape and material. The Chin have an oboe-like instrument, the *bu-hne*, which consists of a gourd holding a number of bamboo or reeds. The Mon gong circle is a curved horseshoe

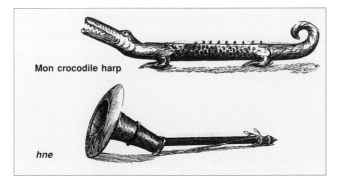

Mon crocodile harp

hne

shape lined with gongs. The Kayah have a bamboo flute with different lengths of bamboo attached to each other in a triangular shape.

LITERATURE

The earliest Burmese literature was mainly of a religious nature and inscribed on stone. These inscriptions go as far back as the Pagan period in the 11th century.

Palm leaf manuscripts and folded paper manuscripts came into existence only after the 15th century. The literature during this period was mainly concerned with the *Jataka* tales told by the Buddha to his disciples in answer to certain questions, and were in the forms of drama and epistles or missives, written in verse. Works on law and history were written in prose. Many dramas were written during the 16th to 18th centuries while during the 19th century, poems, drama and chronicles were written.

After Burma fell to the British, Burmese literature began to feel the impact of a western culture; the arrival of the printing press also influenced literature, which previously had been written for a much smaller audience. Plays which had been written for the court were now available to a wider audience; these plays were not performed on the stage, but were meant to be read. Novels followed plays, the first Burmese novel being an adaptation of Alexander Dumas' *The Count of Monte Cristo*, in a Burmese setting.

Burmese classical literature is of a flowery style with difficult and long sentences, and is concerned with the supernatural and magical. Originating from the court of the Burmese kings, it was greatly influenced by Buddhist Pali and Sanskrit sources.

Khin Myo Chit, literally "Nation Loving Maid," a novelist and author of many books on Burmese culture and oral traditions, writes in both Burmese and English. Her works have been published at home and abroad.

MYAZEDI INSCRIPTION

The Myazedi inscription is a four-sided stone inscription executed in 1113 by Prince Rajakumara recording the merit of the building of a pagoda in Pagan by the prince for his dying father, King Kyansittha. The inscription is written in Burmese, Pyu, Mon and Pali and was discovered in 1887. The discovery of this inscription proved that Burmese was used in the Pagan period and permitted the deciphering of the Pyu language, which had not been possible previously.

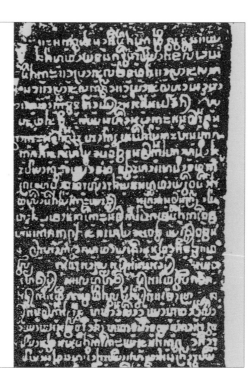

After independence, the Sarpay Beikman, or "Palace of Literature," was set up by the government to promote literature. This institute holds literary seminars, discussions and book exhibitions, makes literary awards, and undertakes translations, research and compilation work. It also operates a book club and publishes an encyclopedia in Burmese.

Modern Burmese literature can be said to have had its beginnings in the 1930s when the University of Rangoon was founded and the Department of Burmese established. A new movement in literature known as the Khitsan movement emerged whose writers used a simple and direct style which has continued to this day. Present day literature is still dominated by religious works, although there are many novels, short stories, poems, children's books, translations of foreign works, and works on culture, art and science. Popular fiction consists mainly of romantic novels and *thaing kung fu* (Burmese martial art) novels.

Literary awards are presented annually. Many well known writers are retired government staff, some of whom have worked or are working in the university. Most writers have a permanent job and write during their spare time.

CRAFTS

In Burma, craftsmen and artisans are still able to make a living in spite of gradual industrialization. Among Burma's many crafts are silk and cotton weaving, lacquerware, gold and silverwork, wood and ivory carving, mosaics, tapestry making, stone carving, boat making, umbrellas and pottery.

A master craftsman.

The cotton and silk *longyi* which Burmese men and women still wear, despite the growing popularity of western dress among the young, are handwoven. Arakan is famous for cotton woven *longyi* in the beautiful *acheik* design, of twisted chains and spirals. Mandalay, Amarapura and Prome are also famous for cotton woven fabric while Mudon, near Moulmein, is known for its cotton woven tablecloths and blankets. Fabric for silk *longyi* is woven in Mandalay and Amarapura, and the Shan States. A favorite design is the beautiful multicolored *Lun-ta-ya*, or Hundred Shuttles. Other handwoven items include shawls and blankets from Pakkoku in northeastern Burma, and shoulder bags from Shan and Kachin, the last woven on a small loom held with the feet.

Tapestries, known as *kalagar* are popular tourist purchases and are made of appliqué designs on velvet or cotton cloth with glass beads and sequins stitched in. These are traditional designs of dancers, peacocks, elephants and mythical animals.

Lacquerware is an ancient craft called *yun* after the Yuns of north Thailand from whom the Burmese learned the craft. Pagan and Prome are lacquerware producing areas. Typical articles are ashtrays, trinket boxes, vases, bowls, tables and chests. The process involves coating a framework of woven bamboo with *thit-see* (raw lacquer obtained from a tree) and clay. The article is dried, after which there are several other coatings. Finally, a design is hand-painted on the article.

Gold leaf is regularly placed on the surface of pagodas as a form of worship. The gold leaf industry is located in Mandalay. Gold is pounded until it is very thin and placed between thick bamboo paper and packed for sale at pagodas. Golden ornaments set with gems are worn by Burmese women and treated as a form of investment. There are goldsmiths in every town where women come to sell and buy jewelry, and also to reset old jewelry in modern designs.

Silverware was once very well known. Burmese women wore silver belts and silver bowls were used by the well-to-do for weddings and festivals. But these articles are slowly getting more difficult to find in Burmese homes, as owners sell them to supplement their incomes.

Pottery-making in Burma consists of plain earthenware for cooking pots, flower pots and water pots; glazed ware for water jars, flower vases, pickle jars; and miscellaneous small glazed articles such as ashtrays and pencil holders.

A craft much related to religion is the making of Buddha images, either carved from marble or cast in brass, copper or silver. Marble Buddha images are carved in Mandalay while brass, copper and silver Buddha images are made at Ywataung near Mandalay.

Left: **Karen weaver.**

Below: **A lacquer *lepet* box.**

Games played with hands are numerous: in *kyet-pyan-nghet-pyan* (hens fly birds fly), children sit in a circle, placing their hands, palms downward, on the ground. The leader shouts *"kyet-pyan-nghet-pyan"* and calls out the names of flying, or non-flying, animals or objects; all must raise their hands for flying objects. The person who does not raise his hand for a flying object, or raises his hand for a non-flying object, loses.

LEISURE

GAMES

CHILDREN in Burma play games in the shade of trees in the evening cool and even at night by the light of the full moon.

One game, the *toke-see-toe*—played with two teams, one team guarding lines or rows that the other team tries to pass through—is usually played on full moon nights because it involves a lot of running and perspiration!

Most Burmese children can find enough ingenuity and imagination to turn old flat sardine cans into cars by tying a string and pulling them around. Old bicycle tire rims are rolled along with a stick; banana leaves and stems can be made into toy guns, rings, and bangles. Slingshots are easily made by carving a small piece of wood into a Y shape and tying a piece of rubber tubing to it. Pellets are made from mud from river banks, patiently rolled into small balls and dried in the sun.

Kites are flown in fields, the string rubbed with starch and glass powder, so sharp that they can cut hands and even blind eyes! On a windy day kites are flown with the main purpose of bringing down another kite by cutting it adrift.

On the tamer side, draughts, or checkers, can be played with bottle caps on cardboard boards. Grannies teach grandchildren to fold paper into ships, boats and other objects. With so many kinds of games and playthings there is almost no need for dolls and electronic toys!

In *phan-kone-dan*, two children sit on the ground with legs stretched out and soles touching. Other children jump over this obstacle which gets higher and higher as the children pile one foot on top of another.

SPORTS

Soccer is Burma's favorite sport. The spectators at national league soccer matches always fill the national Aung San stadium, often overflowing into the streets around the stadium. During the 1960s and 1970s Burma's national team was foremost in Southeast Asia, but in recent years it has sadly declined in performance. Soccer is played from boyhood with any kind of ball, and especially on rainy days, a match is very exciting, not to say muddy!

Chinlone, a traditional game once played to entertain the king, is a popular sport in Burma played in proper courts and watched by many, or in the streets by young boys.

Chinlone is a traditional sport played with a cane ball. The ball, made of rattan cane, is hollow inside, and about sixteen inches in circumference. Usually, six players stand in a circle and try to keep the ball in the air by using only knees, heels, toes, elbows, shoulders and head, but not the hands. It is a simple game but requires great skill and good teamwork in tossing the ball around. *Chinlone* was once a game played to entertain the king, but it declined in popularity during the colonial period. In the post-independence period there have been great efforts to revive and promote it and there are now many *chinlone* associations and even women players who are so skilled that they can keep several cane balls going at once. A variation of *chinlone* is played like volleyball, over a net, with two teams participating.

Burmese boxing looks very violent even to most Burmese spectators. The boxers are allowed to use any part of the body to fight, and the match is won by the person who draws first blood. Each boxer is allowed to wipe blood away three times before being declared the loser. A number of rules such as trimmed nails and no kicking in the groin, scratching or biting have to be observed. The boxer's class is not determined by body weight, but by skill. A youngster begins in the lowest fourth class and moves up when he gets too good for his opponents in the same class. In matches, fighters are matched by weight and build within their own class. However, when a boxer reaches the first class, he has to take on all comers. Boxing matches featuring famous boxers travel from town to town and can be found at pagoda festivals. Boxing matches are accompanied by a Burmese orchestra. Matches usually take place after the harvest until just before the rainy season.

Thaing is a Burmese martial art and a form of self-defense. Players may use long swords called *dah* in one form of *thaing*. In recent years it has been greatly popularized in movies, comic strips and novels featuring the heroes of the days of the kings, just as *kung fu* and karate have in the west.

In the villages, cockfighting is still found. It is a cruel sport with the cocks wearing sharp spurs. The spectators place bets as in any other sport.

Western sports such as tennis, golf, volleyball, basketball and badminton are played in urban areas, but some sports like cricket, American football and baseball are not widely known. Rowing, yachting, table tennis, bicycling and hiking are also sports which have a number of enthusiasts in the capital city of Rangoon. Burma's track and field record in Southeast Asia has been outstanding, especially in the marathon.

Burmese boxing is a violent sport in which the victor is the boxer who draws first blood.

STORYTELLING

Stories are told by grandparents, aunts, elder sisters and cousins to younger children to keep them quiet and to teach them good morals such as honesty, diligence, generosity and faith, and also to show that evil comes to the wicked. Most children love stories and favorite storyteller-aunts and cousins on a visit may be pestered until they give in with a story or two! There are so many kinds of stories to be told—folk tales, ethnic tales, humorous tales, tales of kings, queens, princes and princesses, and most important of all, the *Jataka* tales and the Dhammapada, tales from the Buddha's life.

A grandmother tells stories to younger children to keep them quiet and teach them good morals.

Folk tales are handed down by word of mouth from generation to generation, and they tell of Master Golden Rabbit, Master Tiger, Master Fox and other animals whose adventures are funny and full of lessons to be learned. Master Simpleton, Mr. and Mrs. Deaf and Mr. Clever are some of the typical characters of folk tales.

Ethnic tales are told to preserve ethnic legends about the origins of each group, as well as its festivals and customs, while humorous tales are earthy, some of which would not be mentioned in other societies, but are accepted as natural and worthy of a hearty laugh! Tales of kings and life at court tell of heroes famous for their strength and courage and their perseverance in the face of danger and in seemingly hopeless situations.

THE RABBIT'S COLD

Once upon a time a lion lived in a cave. His loyal subjects were the Bear, the Monkey and the Rabbit. One day the Lion hit upon an idea to obtain food easily. First of all he called the Bear to him, opened his mouth wide and asked him to tell him what kind of smell the Bear could smell. The Bear said, "Oh, Lion, I smell the smell of rotten meat." "What!" said the Lion, "do you dare to say that to me, the King of the Forest?" So saying, he bit the Bear and ate him up.

Next he turned to the Monkey and asked him the same question. Having seen what had happened to the honest Bear the Monkey said, "Oh, Lion, your mouth has the fragrance of lilies." "What!" said the Lion, "I who live on the meat of lesser animals cannot possibly have such fragrance issuing from my mouth! Do you dare to lie to me?" So the Monkey went the same way as the Bear.

Last was the Rabbit's turn. The Rabbit did not come up close to the Lion but said, "Oh, Lion, I have such a very bad cold and my nose cannot detect any smell whatever. Allow me to go home and cure my cold first, please." With that the Rabbit ran away as fast as he could and never went near the Lion's cave again.

A CONTEST OF TALL TALES

Once upon a time three young men lived in a village near a crossroads. One day they saw a well-dressed stranger resting in a *zayat* (a resting place) at the crossroads. Coveting his fine clothes, they went up to the stranger and invited him to a contest of tall tales; the person who did not believe a tale was to be the loser and to become the servant of the storyteller.

The first young man said, "When I was in my mother's womb I wanted to eat some sour plums so much. So I left my mother's body, went into the forest and climbed a plum tree where I ate to my heart's content. The plums were so sour my teeth ached. Then when I was about to descend I found I didn't know how to get down. So I went home, brought a ladder and finally got to the ground. Then I stole back into my mother's womb. Well, do you all believe my story?"

No one shook his head so the second man continued, "It was when I was a year old, and I went out hunting rabbits. I came upon a tiger. It was so big but I went up to him, opened his mouth wide with my two bare hands and the tiger split in two." Again the listeners nodded their belief.

Then it was the third youth's turn, "I was seven days old and wanted so much to eat fish. So I went to the river to fish. Since I did not catch any fish until noon, I dived to the bottom of the river. I found there a fish as large as a mountain. I boxed the fish, then made a fire and roasted the fish and ate it. Then I floated up to the river's surface and went home." Once again all nodded that they believed this tale.

The last story was told by the stranger, "About 15 years ago, I owned a cotton field. The drought that year was so bad all the trees died except for one which bore three enormous bolls. Three young men emerged from these and I bathed them and took them home. They worked for me but one day they ran away. I have looked far and wide for them and only now have I found them. Those three youths are the three of you. You believe me, don't you?" At this the three young men bowed their heads in silence; either way they had lost the contest. The stranger, however, did not take them with him as his servants but merely took their clothes and went on his way.

FESTIVALS

BURMESE CALENDAR

The Burmese calendar consists of 12 lunar months. The difference between the lunar year and the solar year is made up for by the addition of an extra month every few years. The Burmese year, 1351, begins in mid-March, 1989, and ends in mid-March, 1990. For religious matters, the Burmese use the Buddhist calendar, which is also the lunar calendar, but the calculation begins from the year of Buddha's Enlightenment: 1989 is the year 2533 on the Buddhist calendar. There is a festival for each Burmese month beginning from the first month of Tagu.

Burmese months	Corresponding English months:
Tagu	mid-March to mid-April
Kasone	mid-April to mid-May
Nayone	mid-May to mid-June
Waso	mid-June to mid-July
Wagaung	mid-July to mid-August
Tawthalin	mid-August to mid-September
Thadingyut	mid-September to mid-October
Tazaungmone	mid-October to mid-November
Nadaw	mid-November to mid-December
Pyatho	mid-December to mid-January
Tabodwei	mid-January to mid-February
Tabaung	mid-February to mid-March

Opposite: **Child clowns dance at a pagoda festival procession.**

WATER FESTIVAL

The Water Festival, lasting four to five days, is celebrated in mid-April to welcome the Burmese New Year. During this time the Burmese throw water on each other; the amount of water varies from a sprinkle of a few drops of perfumed water to bowls—and bucketfuls.

Special structures called *pandal* are constructed at the side of main roads. These are usually open-sided with bamboo poles supporting the bamboo-strip matting used for the roof. In front of the *pandal*, water barrels and pipes are lined up. During the festival, the people participate either by throwing water at one of the *pandal*, or going from *pandal* to *pandal* in open jeeps, small or large trucks or buses, to have water thrown on them. Each *pandal* has pretty, young, brightly dressed girls lined up as early as 8 a.m., ready to throw water.

Water-throwing is for the young, however. The elderly do not participate in the fun but, instead, go to monasteries or meditation centers for quiet meditation.

On the last day, New Year's Day, no more water is thrown. The Burmese welcome the New Year by setting free fish, birds and cattle. The elders have their hair washed by the younger folk. Special feasts are given to the monks in the monasteries.

At the height of activity, it gets riotous as groups do battle with their hoses! The Water Festival symbolically washes away the old year's bad luck and sins, and it also serves the practical purpose of cooling everyone when temperatures soar as high as 100°F or more. It is a time of great fun, practical jokes are played on strangers, passersby are made fun of and no one is allowed to get angry. It is a time to get rid of inhibitions and grievances.

BANYAN TREE-WATERING CEREMONY

In every pagoda and monastery in Burma, a banyan tree is planted because it was under the banyan tree that the Buddha attained Enlightenment. On the full moon day of Kasone, the second month of the Burmese calendar, a sacred day to the Buddhist—it was on this day that the Buddha was born, later attained Enlightenment, and finally died —the banyan tree is watered by worshipers in a ceremony. Worshipers, carrying earthen water pots, take turns to water the tree, whose base is enclosed in a decorative concrete structure.

At the banyan tree-watering ceremony, worshipers carrying earthen water pots take turns to water the tree.

WASO ROBE-OFFERING CEREMONY

Dhamma-set-kya Day, the full moon day of Waso, the fourth month in the Burmese calendar, commemorates the preaching of the Buddha's first sermon forty-nine days after his Enlightenment. This day also marks the beginning of the Buddhist Lent which lasts for the three months of the rainy season. A robe-offering ceremony is performed not later than the full moon day of Waso, as during Lent the monks are required to spend the period at their monasteries and forbidden to travel; the robes offered are for their use during this period of retreat.

For the people, Lent is a quiet time of restraint with few social activities; weddings are not celebrated, and people prefer not to move house.

FESTIVAL OF LIGHTS

The Festival of Lights is celebrated at the end of Lent on the full moon day of Thadingyut, which coincides with the end of the rainy season. This festival commemorates the descent of Buddha to earth after preaching to his divine mother in heaven for the three months of Lent, the Buddhist Abidhamma, the most difficult of Buddhist teachings. Buddhist homes light up at night with paper lanterns hung on front porches, or simply with candles; government offices and buildings are decorated with colorful electric lights. The festival lasts three days, from the eve of the full moon to the day after the full moon.

Since this festival marks the end of Lent it is a time of great joy with some streets being closed off at night and stages erected at one end, for all-night performances by dancers, comedians, singers and musicians. Small stalls sell local foods and handicrafts.

It is the custom for the younger people to show their respect and gratitude to parents, teachers and mentors by going to their homes with gifts of cakes, fruits and so on. In making these offerings, they sit at floor level, and make the gesture of obeisance three times, while the elders give suitable blessings for good health, wealth and safe passage through life.

The Shwe Dagon is a fairyland of lights on the night of the Festival of Lights, which is celebrated at the end of the Buddhist Lent.

KAHTEIN ROBE-OFFERING CEREMONY

The Kahtein robe-offering ceremony is performed during the month of Tazaungmone. Robes and other articles are offered to monks; feasts are also held, with many guests invited to take part in the merit-making.

A second Festival of Lights is held at this time, a month after the first Festival of Lights; again it lasts three days from the eve of the full moon day to the day after the full moon.

At Rangoon's Shwe Dagon pagoda, an all-night weaving contest takes place where weavers spend the night weaving robes which must be completed at dawn, when the robes are offered to the Buddha images at the pagoda. Similarly, other such all-night weaving takes place around the country.

On the full moon night there is the custom of hiding other people's possessions in various places as a joke, for example moving the neighbors' flower pots or water barrels, or removing the washing line.

The donors of *hta-ma-ne* personally prepare it at the monastery where they are making the offering, to the monks.

HTA-MA-NE MAKING FESTIVAL

This festival celebrates the harvest and takes place in the month of Tabodwei. *Hta-ma-ne* is made from glutinous rice, peanuts, ginger, oil, garlic, sesame seed and coconut. The ginger, garlic and coconut are sliced finely and added to the glutinous rice, and the mixture cooked in large pans over open fires in monastery grounds or private gardens. The mixture is so sticky that it has to be stirred by grown men with big wooden paddles. This rich and fragrant pudding is given to all visitors.

In the month of Tawthalin, a unique pagoda festival takes place in Inle Lake in eastern Burma. Here, on and around Inle Lake, the Inthas live, weaving silk and cotton, fishing and growing vegetables on floating gardens. They go about in boats either rowed with oars or propelled by outboard motors; the rowing is done in a standing position with one leg wrapped around the oar, hence the "leg rowers of Inle Lake."

During the Hpaung-daw-u Pagoda Festival, three Buddha images from the pagoda are taken round in lovely decorated boats on the lake so that the people can worship from their own boats as the Buddha images pass by.

PAGODA FESTIVALS

Burma is a land of pagodas and the more famous pagodas have their own festival day. The Shwe Dagon Pagoda Festival is held around the full moon day of Tabaung, the last month of the year.

Pagoda festivals have ferris wheels, all-night shows and dances, and stalls selling food, local handicrafts and souvenirs. Villagers from all around will come, spending the night watching shows, eating favorite delicacies, going home only in the morning, in their bullock carts.

ETHNIC FESTIVALS

Each of the ethnic groups in Burma has its own festivals. Of these the better known festivals are Karen New Year, Kachin Manao Festival and Pa-o Rocket Firing Festivals.

KAREN NEW YEAR Karen New Year is celebrated on the new moon day of the lunar month, Pyatho, which falls around mid-December to mid-January. This day is a national holiday. In Rangoon, Karens gather at various communal centers and *Don* dances are performed by Karen girls and boys wearing Karen dress. In Pa-an, the capital of the Karen State, the *Don* is performed with great ceremony. Frog drums and buffalo horns are played.

KACHIN MANAO FESTIVAL The Kachins celebrate a victory or a prosperous period, or mark the illness or death of parents or the moving away of a family member with a Manao Festival.

The Manao Festival involves great expense, as there is a vast number of guests. Only chieftains (*duwa*) are capable of bearing the expense; one such festival involved the slaughtering of 14 buffaloes, 20 cows, 20 pigs and 50 chickens, 200 baskets of rice and 4,500 bottles of spirits! A large shelter, decorated with a huge pair of buffalo horns, is built with four *manao* poles in the center; drinking, eating and dancing are held here. The *manao* poles are kept for a whole year.

The *Don* dance is performed by Karen boys and girls during the Karen New Year.

111

A traditional kitchen.

112

FOOD

KITCHENS

BURMESE KITCHENS are presided over by the female members of the household, such as the mother, elder daughters, aunts or grandmothers.

In the kitchen, a low round table about one and a half feet in height is used, with low stools as seats. Common kitchen articles in Burmese kitchens are a mortar and pestle of stone, a chopping block, usually a round cross-section of a tree trunk, earthen or aluminum pots without handles and earthen water jars. Wood or charcoal fires are used, as electricity is available only in larger urban areas and kerosene is scarce.

Most of the kitchen activity takes place at floor level. Because the meat and vegetables are bought without benefit of storage or packaging, a lot of cleaning has to be done after their purchase. For this, and the cleaning of large pots, a corner of the kitchen is separated by a low raised kerb on which one squats while washing. Sometimes, washing is done outside the kitchen, in the backyard, where water is stored in large barrels of wood or metal.

Burmese households use a *kyaung-ein*, or "cat safe," to keep cooked foods, leftovers, crockery, cutlery, miscellaneous spices and ingredients in bottles. The safe is a small wooden cupboard about four to five feet high, a foot deep and about two feet wide. The sides and front are of wire mesh to give proper airing for the food inside; a couple of drawers provide space for cutlery.

A "cat safe."

Spices are important ingredients in Burmese cooking.

MAIN INGREDIENTS

Rice, being a staple, features in most meals and snacks. Rice is eaten as a salad, fried, cooked with coconut cream, or kneaded with fish. Glutinous rice is steamed, boiled or rolled in banana leaves with banana stuffing. Rice flours are used in many dishes, cakes and desserts.

Burmese add many spices and herbs in their cooking, including fresh ones. Turmeric, chilli, onions, garlic and ginger are pounded in a stone mortar and cooked in oil to obtain fragrance before meat, fish or vegetable is added. Coriander leaf, lemon grass, tamarind juice, fish sauce and fish paste are included in many dishes.

Burmese women cook without the help of strict recipes. Recipes are handed down through generations by word of mouth and one learns by doing rather than reading. However, during the last decade Burmese recipe books have gained popularity.

Burmese also eat western bread, cakes and cookies, but wheat flour and other baking ingredients are scarce and western cakes are only for special occasions. Gifts of cakes are given to parents and elders on festival days as a mark of respect.

MEAT, VEGETABLES AND FRUIT All kinds of meat are eaten by the Burmese, but most prefer fish, fish products and shrimp. If meat is avoided, it is usually beef because the cow, used to plow the soil for rice, is regarded as a benefactor. Buddhists believe the slaughter of a large animal for its meat is more sinful than that of a smaller one; in offering food to monks, certain meats are prohibited including bear, elephant, snake and tiger meat. Some monks are vegetarian although there is no specific religious taboo on meat. Many lay people avoid meat during the months of Buddhist Lent from July to October.

Burmese like to eat raw or blanched vegetables with fish sauce dips, and drink soups made from freshly plucked tender leaves of certain tropical trees and shrubs. They enjoy eating the roselle leaf, a sour tasting vegetable, as well as water greens, the leaves of an aquatic morning glory. Okra, drumsticks, gourd, chayote and brinjals are

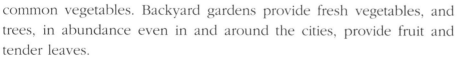

common vegetables. Backyard gardens provide fresh vegetables, and trees, in abundance even in and around the cities, provide fruit and tender leaves.

Because of the varied climate in the different regions of Burma, a wide variety of tropical and temperate vegetables and fruit is available. Fruits such as strawberries, avocados and oranges were introduced in the colonial period while grapefruit and apples were introduced as late as the 1950s. Common local fruits are mango, durian, mangosteen, rambutan, tangerine, pear, watermelon and jackfruit. Burmese like to eat fruit peeled and cut to savor the taste of each individual fruit. Mixed fruit salads are not common.

Burmese still use leaves to wrap food; broad leaves such as banana leaves are used in the bazaar to wrap purchases of fish, meat and vegetables. Banana leaves sometimes serve as plates at a feast. To enhance the flavor of traditional cakes, banana, bamboo and palm leaves are used as wrappers when cooking; the juice of *pandan* leaves is used for fragrance and color.

115

TRADITIONAL BURMESE FARE

Since Burma lies between India and China, both Indian and Chinese influences can be found in Burmese cuisine. Many Burmese dishes are cooked in a Chinese manner, including stir-frying, and the use of bean curd, bean sprouts and soy sauce. Indian influence can be seen in the use of spices for chicken curries. On special occasions, Burmese serve *biryani*, an Indian dish, chicken cooked with spices in saffron rice.

A traditional main meal consists of boiled rice, a soup, a salad, a curry of meat or fish, and vegetables, eaten raw with fish paste sauce, boiled or fried. In rural areas, the curry may be served only occasionally.

For breakfasts, most Burmese like to eat *mohinga*, rice noodles in a fish soup. Certain towns in Burma are famous for different types of *mohinga*. Glutinous rice steamed with toasted dried fish, sesame powder and grated coconut is also a favorite. Another breakfast favorite is *naan*, an Indian wheat bread, eaten with boiled beans tossed in an oil and salt dressing. Fried rice made from leftover rice from the evening before also makes an adequate breakfast. Bread is eaten only in the main urban areas, and then, not every day.

In a traditional main meal, each person is served a plate of boiled rice; the other dishes that accompany the rice are placed at the center of the table, and are shared by all.

Left: **Making jaggery, a favorite dessert, in Hmawza village.**

Below: **Lepet is pickled tea leaf eaten as a savory snack with dried shrimps, peanuts, sesame seed, fried garlic, and fried beans with an oil and salt dressing. The pickled tea leaves are first marinated in oil and pounded garlic. With lepet, one usually drinks plain tea. This snack is served at feasts and in homes to visitors. Older folk like to eat just plain lepet as it is believed to have medicinal properties.**

SNACKS, SALADS AND DESSERTS Snacks are usually fritters of onions, beans, bananas or gourd, a large green fruit obtained from the gourd vine.

Burmese salads are made of raw or boiled vegetables or meat mixed with sliced onion, garlic, dried shrimp powder, ground peanuts, roasted bean powder, fish sauce, lime or tamarind juice, and oil, cooked with turmeric to remove the oily taste.

Dessert may be fruit peeled and cut, fruit preserves, nuts or jaggery, or palm sugar balls, served with plain tea (that is, without milk or sugar). Traditional desserts are made from coconut, rice or glutinous rice flour, and jaggery. Coconut cream is an essential ingredient in traditional Burmese desserts.

DRINKS

Alcohol is avoided by most Burmese who are devout Buddhists, except perhaps for rare social occasions and in urban areas. Drinking of alcohol in any form is generally regarded as an indication of poor morals and constitutes a violation of basic Buddhist precepts. However, a traditional wine made from toddy palm or *dani* (a palm which grows in swamps) is drunk by rural folk as a pastime or at festivals.

The only drink at the end of a meal is water from a water pot kept on a three-legged stand, or Burmese tea. Coffee or tea is drunk at breakfast or sometimes in the afternoon, in a ready-mix brew with condensed milk. Soft drinks are served on special occasions.

ROADSIDE WATER POT STAND

The gift of water holds special significance for Buddhists who believe it brings ten merits: longevity, beauty, riches, strength, knowledge, cleanliness, fame, friends, never being in need of water, and being swift as flowing water.

Buddhists offer water to the Buddha in household shrines, dig wells, and build water pot stands for thirsty travelers, to gain religious merit. These small stands are of wood and are four-legged, with a roof to give cover to the pots and cups. The base around the pot is sometimes filled with sand which keeps the water cool, and bright green paddy seedlings growing in the sand lighten the heart of the weary.

MEALTIMES

Mealtimes in Burmese families are earlier than western mealtimes. In rural areas the family wakes before dawn, at about 4 a.m., and breakfast in the fields would be at about 5 or 6 a.m. In the urban areas, breakfast is at about 7 a.m. The midday meal is taken at about noon; office workers carry their own food to the office in a small lunch box or tiered tiffin carrier (see illustration). Afternoon tea or coffee is substituted by a main meal at about 5 p.m. In urban areas where there is no night life, a light snack with a pot of Burmese tea might be sufficient for supper before bedtime at 10 or 11 p.m. Bedtime is even earlier in villages due to lack of electricity and other lighting fuel.

Office workers carry their lunches to work in tiered tiffin carriers.

COMMON FOOD TABOOS AND BELIEFS

Watermelons should never be eaten with duck eggs.
Ice potato, a root from a bean vine, should not be eaten with chocolate or candy.
Mangosteen must not be eaten with sugar.
Sour foods must not be eaten after drinking milk and eating milk products.
Durians must be eaten with mangosteen to offset the heating effect of durians.
Drumstick tree leaves are good for high blood pressure.
Pickled tea leaves (*lepet*) help keep one awake.
Crocodile meat must not be cooked with turmeric.

TABLE MANNERS

The Burmese do not dine in the western sense of savoring food or wines and making conversation. The meal is quickly eaten, and is over when one is full. There is no lingering at the dinner table, and guests may leave quite soon after eating. Dishes are flavorous, but there is no emphasis on decoration or garnish. A meal does not consist of courses. Instead the dishes are placed in the center of the kitchen table, usually a low round table, with the diners seated on smooth bamboo mats. In urban houses there are western-type dining tables and chairs. There is no specific seating arrangement. Portions from all the dishes are placed in one's plate and eaten with rice.

A Shan family sits down to a meal at home. Burmese eat with their fingers.

The most important eating etiquette is to serve the head of the family or oldest member first. Even if this person is not present at the time, it is customary to reserve the first portion for him. If fingers are used, and many Burmese feel that eating this way is more conducive to hearty enjoyment of the meal, then the fingers must, of course, be washed first.

Generally, there is not much conversation during the meal. Talking with one's mouth full, singing, talking about topics such as body wastes, making noises, and so on, are avoided. Eating too slowly, lying down and lazing, and singing are regarded as being disrespectful of the meal.

If there are guests, they should be pressed to have some more food, and, even if they refuse, the host may insist on serving them another portion.

DRINKING CUSTOMS

Burmese mainly avoid alcohol and there are no drinking customs as such among them.

Ethnic Burmans drink toddy wine or *dani* wine while most of the other ethnic groups drink wine made from rice or glutinous rice. A cheap home brew called country spirit or "CS" is made from rice or corn and drunk all over the country.

Among the ethnic groups, the Chin people who live in the western mountains drink a sweet wine, *khaung yei*. They have the custom of drinking wine with a friend from the same container, usually a bamboo section. *Hlaw sa*, the fermented rice from which *khaung yei* is extracted, can be eaten as a kind of pudding.

Ethnic groups celebrate festivities with drinking. At the Kachin Manao Festival it is said that up to 3,000 bottles of *khaung yei* and 1,500 bottles of country spirit are needed for the numerous guests. The Pa-o people also drink in celebration before the Rocket-firing Festival. Ethnic Karens drink at funerals and at bone collecting ceremonies.

In the Shan State, unlike the rest of Burma, liquor is sold and consumed freely.

Two Chin men sharing wine from the same bamboo container.

FEASTS

For the Burmese, a feast usually involves an offering of food and other items to monks, with the guests arriving later. Such feasts may take place in one's own home or at a monastery. The number of guests varies from a few close relatives to hundreds of guests arriving at staggered intervals through a whole morning. The occasion for a feast may be a birthday, a Buddhist initiation or ear-piercing ceremony, a christening, a wedding anniversary, or to make merit for one's deceased parents, or for oneself, such as donation of a new building to a monastery, offering of robes on festival days, and so on.

If the feast is held in one's home, the night before the feast is one of great activity. The living room has to be cleared of chairs and tables, and carpets or smooth mats laid out, a special place for the monks being reserved. If the food to be offered is cooked at home, a small army of cooks made up of relatives—with a repertoire of tasty dishes—and a number of volunteer helpers may be seen peeling and

When a feast is being held, relatives pitch in to help with the cooking.

At a feast, offerings of robes and presents are made to monks who are then invited to a sumptuous meal (below), after which the other guests are served (left).

cleaning the onions, garlic and ginger. The food to be cooked has already been collected in several marketing trips. The food is cooked during the night; the pots are so big that a wood fire has to be built outside, in the backyard. In the villages, all the villagers or neighbors may come to help or at least give the support of their presence. If the feast is held in a monastery, it is customary to order the food or have it cooked on the grounds by staff from the monastery.

When the monks arrive, they are offered the food, after which a suitable sermon is delivered and certain *sutras* chanted in order to bestow on the audience the benefits of protection from danger, illness and misfortunes. The host and hostess share their merit with all beings, and guests praise the act by saying *sadhu* three times. Then the guests are served food.

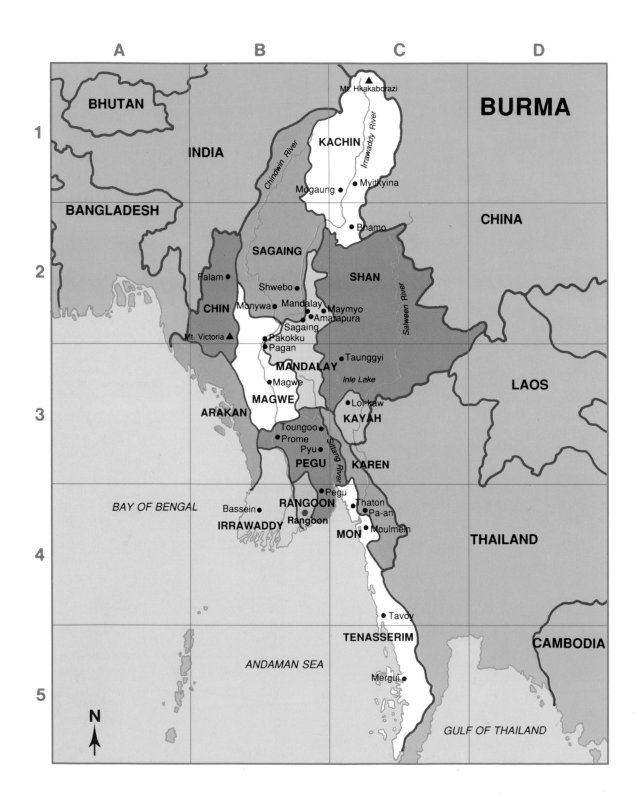

A B C D

BHUTAN

INDIA

BANGLADESH

BURMA

1

▲ Mt. Hkakaborazi

KACHIN

Chindwin River

Irrawaddy River

Mogaung ● ● Myitkyina

CHINA

● Bhamo

2

SAGAING

Falam ●

SHAN

CHIN

Shwebo ●

Monywa ● Mandalay ● ● Maymyo
Sagaing ● Amarapura
Pakokku ●
Mt. Victoria ▲ ● Pagan

Salween River

MANDALAY

● Taunggyi

Inle Lake

3

● Magwe

MAGWE

LAOS

ARAKAN

● Lol-kaw

KAYAH

Toungoo ●
Prome ● Pyu ●

Sittang River

KAREN

PEGU

BAY OF BENGAL

Bassein ●

Pegu ●

RANGOON

● Rangoon

Thaton ●
Pa-an ●

IRRAWADDY

MON

● Moulmein

THAILAND

4

● Tavoy

TENASSERIM

CAMBODIA

ANDAMAN SEA

5

● Mergui

N

GULF OF THAILAND

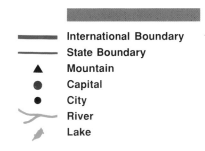

International Boundary
State Boundary
▲ Mountain
● Capital
● City
River
Lake

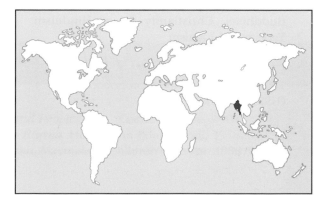

INDEX

Picture Credits

Jon Burbank, Birgitte Dessau,
Alain Evrard, Michael Freeman,
G.A. Grinsted, Peter Korn,
Noazesh Ahmed, Julia Oh,
Harold Pfeiffer, Luca I. Tettoni,
Paul Tracey, Veronique Sanson,
Diane Wilson